HIGHWAY TO HISTORY

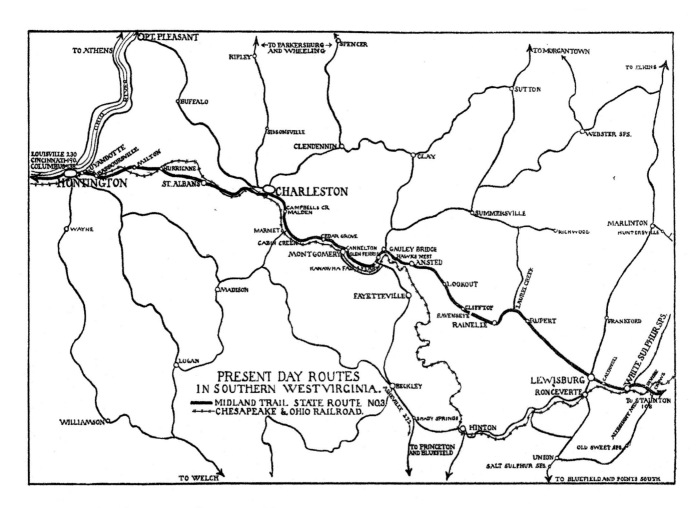

Long before the coming of Interstate 64, this vintage map showed the similar routes of the Midland Trail and the Chesapeake & Ohio Railway.

HIGHWAY TO HISTORY

A Midland Trail Scrapbook

James E. Casto

Quarrier
press

Charleston, West Virginia

Quarrier Press
Charleston, WV

First Edition

10 9 8 7 6 5 4 3 2 1

Printed in China

Library of Congress Control Number: 2011934875
ISBN-13: 978-1-891852-77-0
ISBN-10: 1-891852-77-9

Cover design: Mark S. Phillips
Book design: Mark S. Phillips & Steve Lewis

Distributed by:

West Virginia Book Company
1125 Central Avenue
Charleston, WV 25302
www.wvbookco.com

CONTENTS

AUTHOR'S NOTE

Most of today's motorists prefer to stick to the easier, far quicker driving offered by Interstate 64. But those travelers who are willing to take their time and instead drive the two-lane blacktop of West Virginia's Midland Trail can get a glimpse into history that's denied those who hurry along the super-highway.

The Midland Trail is more than a road; it's a virtual history book. Originally a rude pathway worn by buffalo and the early pioneers, it stretches from White Sulphur Springs westward to Kenova, zigzagging along rivers, over mountains and through lush valleys. Along the way it touches just about every aspect and time period of West Virginia's story—coal mines and chemical plants, Civil War battlefields and historic churches, ancient Native American burial mounds and African-American slave quarters.

Surely the best way to learn about the Midland Trail is to jump in the family car and set off on a personal exploration. The next best thing is take an armchair look such as that offered in these pages.

When I started work on this book, my intentions were modest. I've collected vintage postcards for years and I simply wanted to share some of the colorful cards I've gathered that picture scenes along West Virginia's historic Midland Trail. But once I embarked on my task, I discovered that my card collection had enormous gaps that, if I wanted to do full justice to the Midland Trail story, I somehow would have to fill. And so the result is this volume, a scrapbook that includes a mixture of vintage postcards, old pictures and contemporary photographs.

This is not an in-depth history of the Midland Trail. Such an effort would require a far larger book—and hands more capable than mine. Instead, it's offered as a generous sized sample of the Midland Trail's multi-faceted story. The scenes included here are by design a wide-ranging mix. Some are historically significant, while others are included just for fun.

I'm indebted to the many kind souls who have helped me along the way. My special thanks to the West Virginia Department of Culture and History, the Greenbrier County Convention & Visitors Bureau, the Chimney Corner Ole Country Store, the Charleston *Daily Mail,* the Huntington *Herald-Dispatch,* the Cabell County Public Library and *Huntington Quarterly*.

All of us who are fascinated by the saga of the Midland Trail owe a special debt of thanks to the Midland Trail Scenic Highway Association. Since 1988, the non-profit association has worked hard at luring tourists and others to the legendary road. Working with the West Virginia Division of Highways, the group has erected mileage markers along the road's 180 miles between Kenova and White Sulphur Springs. For more information about the association and the latest travel info, call 304-343-6001 or 866-ROUTE60, or log on to *www.midlandtrail.com*.

If you enjoy these glimpses of West Virginia's Midland Trail, I urge you to take to the road and launch your own personal exploration of this highway to history.

INTRODUCTION

H.O. Via was an early business leader in Huntington, West Virginia. Via first arrived in the city as a young man in 1872, only a few months after it received its official charter from the Legislature. He had bounced his way from White Sulphur Springs to Charleston on a stagecoach and from Charleston continued on to Huntington aboard a train, traveling over the newly laid tracks of the Chesapeake & Ohio Railway.

It took Via three days and nights to travel the 125 miles from White Sulphur to Charleston. A half century later, in the 1920s, he looked back in a newspaper interview and offered some vivid recollections of that long-ago coach trip:

"It was not like riding one of today's modern buses," Via recalled. "Going up one mountain all the male passengers had to get out and walk. The mud was too deep and the hill too steep for the six horses pulling us. There were six of us men and one woman. The woman rode."

Via and his fellow travelers may have found the route uncomfortable but it was the best there was. For years the road from White Sulphur westward was the only way of getting across the mountains to the Kanawha Valley and then on to the Ohio Valley.

It's a road that's had many names—and witnessed more than 200 years of American history.

Over the decades, it's been known as the Buffalo Trail, the Lewis Trail, the Old Virginia State Road, the James River & Kanawha Turnpike, the Midland Trail and, ultimately, U.S. Route 60.

Legend has it that its path was first worn by herds of migrating buffalo. In the spring the buffalo would graze in the lush lowlands, but as spring turned into summer and the days grew steadily hotter, the big animals fled the heat and headed for the mountains, seeking the cooler air there. When autumn gave way to winter and the first wintry blasts began to blow, instinct caused the buffalo to retrace their course, heading down from the mountains to the lowlands. Season after season, decade after decade the enormous herds followed the same path.

The countless hoof prints of the buffalo fashioned a well-defined trail for the region's Native Americans to follow as they hunted for game or ventured to the Kanawha Valley salt licks.

Still later the region's first white settlers followed the same well-worn pathway when they made their way westward across the mountains into what is now West Virginia.

George Washington traveled the trail during his surveying treks to the western frontier of Virginia. And it was Washington who would encourage the state of Virginia to turn the crude trail into a real road.

When Mary Draper Ingles fled her Shawnee captors, she traveled portions of the trail as she made her daring escape. Daniel Boone hiked it. Stagecoaches rumbled along it. During the Civil War soldiers clad in both blue and gray marched it. Booker T. Washington walked it. Collis P. Huntington's C&O Railway eclipsed it until the spread of the automobile revived a need for it.

In 1774, Col. Andrew Lewis marched his 1,200-man army along it from Lewisburg to Point Pleasant, where he defeated Chief Cornstalk. Soon people were calling it the Lewis Trail.

In 1785, the state of Virginia authorized construction of what would become known as the Old State Road, following the route over which Lewis had led his men. By 1791, the improved road had reached the head of navigable waters at Kelly's Creek (present-day Cedar Grove), where travelers could continue westward on the Kanawha by bateaux—small flat-bottomed boats of French design.

By 1800, the Old State Road had reached the Ohio River. But truth to tell, it wasn't much of a road, and the growing commerce of the Kanawha Valley demanded something better.

In 1820, Virginia authorized the private James River Company "to make a convenient road by the most practicable route from the James to the Great Falls of the Kanawha," near present-day Gauley Bridge. By 1829, the legislators had authorized extending the road to the confluence of the Big Sandy River and the Ohio River at present-day Kenova, West Virginia.

This was the historic James River & Kanawha Turnpike, an east-west toll road that would prove to be one of early America's most important roadways, connecting Virginia to the Ohio Valley. The road was graded out to a width of 66 feet and tollgates were established every few miles.

When weekly stagecoach service was established along the road, it soon gave way to "three a week" and eventually the volume of travel forced the stagecoach line to offer daily service.

Stagecoaches pulled by teams of strong horses and carrying passengers and sacks of U.S. Mail shared the road with Conestoga wagons piled high with freight and those poor souls who had to make their way along the turnpike on foot. (This sketch of a coach on the turnpike was drawn by Joseph H. Diss Debar, who in 1863 designed the Great Seal of West Virginia and in 1864 was named the state's first commissioner of immigration.)

The coaches had no springs, were unheated in winter and decidedly hot and uncomfortable in the heat of summer. The road itself was rutted and dusty in the summer and little more than a muddy quagmire after a heavy rain. A winter snow might bring travel to a halt for days or even weeks.

Inns sprouted along the way. Some were little more than crude log cabins, while others were more fancy. Whisky was plentiful and cheap. Those travelers without money to buy a meal or rent a bed for the night had to cook what they had over a campfire and then sleep outside under the stars.

Not surprisingly, both Union and Confederate troops marched along the turnpike during the Civil War—and sometimes burned its bridges.

Completion of the C&O's tracks across West Virginia in 1873 marked the beginning of the end for the James River & Kanawha Turnpike. Stagecoach travel quickly declined. Soon, daily service went back to three trips a week, then one. Finally, it came to a halt. With no toll collections coming in to pay for upkeep, the turnpike degenerated into little more than a series of mud holes connected by deep ruts.

The buffalo and the Native Americans were gone, the white settlers had settled, the freight wagons moved no more cargo and the stagecoaches gathered dust in forgotten livery stables, as people turned to the faster, more comfortable railway coaches for traveling.

But the coming of the automobile would provide the old road a new lease on life. By World War I, it experienced a rebirth as part of the Midland Trail, a transcontinental highway that stretched from Washington, D.C. to California. Signs designating the Midland Trail were first posted in 1913, but paving was still some years away.

The official "Midland Trail Tour Guide," published in 1916, laid out a detailed account of the coast-to-coast route. The guidebook advised its readers:

"To tour by motor car in the United States today is not altogether a joyous performance, but the labor of such travel is more than repaid by the beauties to be seen, by the healthful nature of the pastime and by the knowledge of our institutions and our people which may be gained through this mode of travel."

One gets an idea of "the labor of such travel" when one reads over the list of supplies the guide suggested the long-distance motorist should take along—a list that includes not just tire chains and a towing rope but also a "good shovel" and an ax.

Commenting on the West Virginia portion of the road, the guide noted: "Generally speaking, the roads are by the first of July in very good shape and give the average traveler no trouble." In other words, don't even think of tackling the drive in anything other than mid-summer.

In the 1930s, when the American Automobile Association was finally able to convince state lawmakers to number their roads, the Midland Trail became U.S. 60, the state's first paved and numbered road.

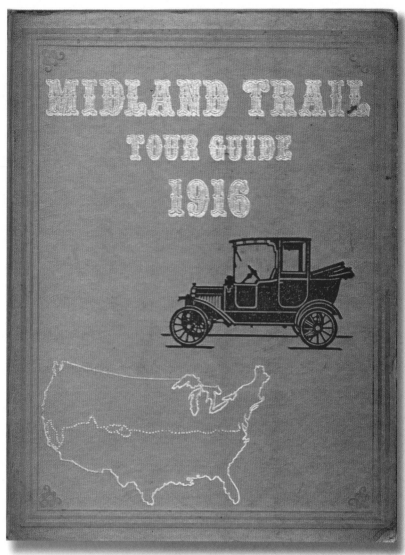

U.S. 60 would serve as the major east-west artery through southern West Virginia until the completion of Interstate 64 in 1988.

In 1989, West Virginia Governor Arch Moore designated U.S. 60 from White Sulphur Springs to Charleston as the Midland Trail Scenic Byway. This original segment became a National Scenic Byway in 2000, and in 2001 the remaining West Virginia portion of U.S. 60 from Charleston to Kenova became a State Scenic Byway.

GREENBRIER COUNTY

As it makes its way across West Virginia, the Midland Trail/U.S. 60 travels through six of the state's 55 counties.

In the east, the first of these is Greenbrier County, the fifth-oldest and second largest county in West Virginia. Formed during the Revolutionary War, on March 1, 1778, from portions of Virginia's Botetourt and Montgomery counties, Greenbrier County is named for the Greenbrier River.

Colonel Andrew Lewis and his father named the river Greenbrier after they encountered prickly green briers while surveying the valley in the mid-1700s. The Greenbrier is a tributary of the New River. At 173 miles in length, it is one of the longest rivers in West Virginia and is said to be the longest untamed (un-dammed) river East of the Mississippi,

Agriculture is important in Greenbrier County. Historically, lumber and coal would be the county's other important industries. Coal mining boomed in parts of the county early in the 20th Century and some mining continues today.

Natural springs appear throughout the county, with several of them supporting thriving resorts in the 19th and early 20th Century. One of those, the Old White at White Sulphur Springs, evolved into The Greenbrier, the world-famed resort.

The population of Greenbrier County in 1820 was 7,340 inhabitants. Families who settled in the county found rich land and abundant game. But the early settlements were frequently the target of bloody raids by Indians who ventured into the area from their camps in the Ohio Valley. Although life was at first not easy, by 1820 the Greenbrier Valley was an established gateway to the new western frontiers of Kentucky, Ohio, and Indiana. *The West Virginia Encyclopedia* quotes one writer of the period as saying that the James River & Kanawha Turnpike—today's Midland Trail/U.S. 60—was a "bustling parade of settlers moving west … tinkers, gypsies, and people just one step ahead of the sheriff."

As the Midland Trail enters West Virginia from Virginia today, it travels the first two miles along Interstate 64, then it branches off the superhighway to descend Allegheny Mountain via U.S. 60's two lanes of blacktop. Thickly forested with pine, hemlock and hardwoods, the ridge forms the watershed between streams flowing eastward to the Atlantic Ocean and westward to the Ohio River and, ultimately, the Gulf of Mexico.

Heading west, the village of White Sulphur Springs, home of The Greenbrier, lies just a bit more than four miles beyond the Virginia line. But just before you get there, you come to one of the roadside oddities that dot the historic highway. In 1959, the late Andy (Tip) Myles built a modern ranch-style house and a small store building from coal. For a number of years the building was home to a souvenir shop.

THE
COAL HOUSE
Built in 1959 by TIP MYLES
30 tons of COAL used in building

NO PARKING
TRESPASSING or
TURNING AROUND
PRIVATE PROPERTY

THE GREENBRIER

By 1827, the James River & Kanawha Turnpike was carrying travelers between Richmond, Virginia, and Charleston, in what is today West Virginia. Many of the weary travelers looked forward to stopping over at White Sulphur Springs to enjoy its mineral waters. This handsome springhouse, a landmark on the grounds of the Greenbrier, may have been built even earlier. When the structure was refurbished, a hollow column was found to contain an 1815 newspaper clipping telling about General Andrew Jackson's victory at New Orleans. Local legend says the springs first attracted attention in 1772 when the invalid wife of an early settler was carried to the spring in a litter. Crippled with rheumatism, she was bathed in a rough trough hollowed out of a tree trunk. She also "drank freely from the fountain" and soon was restored to health.

The White Sulphur Spring, White Sulphur Springs, W. Va. (2,000 Ft. Elevation)

In 1808, James Caldwell erected a tavern at White Sulphur and soon added a dining room, a ballroom and a row of cottages. *West Virginia: A Guide to the Mountain State,* written during the Depression under the sponsorship of the Works Progress Administration, offered an excellent summary of what happened next: "By the 1830s, the resort has become a center of fashion, a favorite rendezvous of elegant plantation society of the Old South. Other rows of cottages were built—Paradise Row, Virginia Row, Georgia Row, Alabama Row, Wolf Row—each with its own social distinctions. Along Paradise Row strutted the young newlyweds and the charming, eager young belles, brought by their families 'to the waters' in the hope of arranging a desirable match."

White Sulphur soon became a popular destination not just for turnpike travelers but also for well-to-do summer vacationers, looking to escape the oppressive heat of the cities. In 1858, this massive three-story resort hotel opened, with 228 guest rooms and a dining room that could seat 1,200. Officially, it was the Grand Central Hotel, but most guests called it "The White" or, in later years, "The Old White." In the Civil War, the hotel was the headquarters of the armies of first one side and then the other, as the battle line moved back and forth across the valley. Later, the resort was pressed into service as a hospital.

The coming of the railroad ushered in a golden age in the West Virginia resort's history. When the Chesapeake & Ohio Railway extended its line through White Sulphur in 1869, the number of guests at The Old White quickly doubled. Above is a rare view of the C&O's White Sulphur station as it looked circa 1903-1905.

This postcard from the 1950s offers an aerial view of The Greenbrier and, at the bottom of the card, the nearby C&O station. Until the decline of rail passenger service, many guests arrived at The Greenbrier by train, sometimes in private rail cars that would be parked on sidings at the station during their owners' stays.

In 1910, the C&O purchased The Old White, paying $150,000 for it. Three years later, the railroad built a modern, Georgian-style building adjacent to it, as shown here. For a few years, the new hotel, christened The Greenbrier, and The Old White operated independently, giving guests a choice between tradition and more modern comforts. At the same time, the resort built its first golf course. Over the years, the words "golf" and "Greenbrier" would become virtually synonymous. In 1922, The Old White failed to meet a state fire inspection and was ordered demolished.

The C&O not only brought golf to The Greenbrier, it also installed tennis courts, horseback trails and other recreational facilities, including this enormous indoor swimming pool. (The pool actually opened in 1912, a year before the hotel was completed.) Responding to demands from guests, the resort set up a polo field. Soon demand forced the installation of a second field. Fencing, indoor archery and golf-driving ranges also were set up.

In 1930-31, at a time when many of the nation's businesses were struggling to survive the impact of the Great Depression, the C&O spent $3.4 million renovating and expanding The Greenbrier. The main structure was expanded from 250 to 580 rooms, a residential wing and an auditorium were added and the dining areas were doubled. This vintage postcard shows the resort's opulent Wisteria Room.

15

Front Facade, Ashford General Hospital, White Sulphur Springs, W. Va. (2,000 Ft. Elevation)

In the wake of the Japanese attack on Pearl Harbor on December 7, 1941, the U.S. State Department used The Greenbrier to house interned Japanese and German diplomats, news correspondents and their families. After six months of difficult negotiations, some 1,400 internees were exchanged for their American counterparts who had been held by the Axis powers. The Greenbrier then reopened for guests, but not for long. In September 1942, the U.S. Army took over. The State Department had leased the hotel, but the Army bought it outright and transformed it into a military installation, named Ashford Hospital. By the war's end, some 25,000 soldiers had been treated at the hospital, shown here in a wartime postcard.

When the Army took over The Greenbrier it agreed in advance to sell the hotel back to the C&O after the war, and at war's end the railroad held the Army to that agreement.

C&O Chairman Robert R. Young hired famed decorator Dorothy Draper to restore the hotel's splendor and she set about doing so, using 30 miles of carpet, 15,000 rolls of wallpaper and 40,000 gallons of paint in the process. This postcard view of the Greenbrier's main lobby offers a glimpse of what might be called "the Dorothy Draper style"—black and white chessboard marble floors, big bold flower prints in drapery, fabric and rugs and elaborate doorway treatments. Draper died in 1969 but the company she founded, now headed by noted designer Carlton Varney, still decorates The Greenbrier.

Kates Mountain Club   White Sulphur Springs, W. Va.

Many of The Greenbrier guests enjoy visiting nearby Kate's Mountain Lodge. Kate's Mountain was named for Kate Carpenter, wife of Nathaniel Carpenter, the region's first pioneer settler, who established "corn rights" to 950 acres by planting them about 1750. Shortly thereafter he was killed in an Indian raid. His wife Kate took refuge on the mountain with her small daughter, later making her way to the nearest fort for safety.

The C&O's former White Sulphur Springs station, located just across the road from The Greenbrier, was converted to retail shopping space some years ago. Nevertheless, a visitor standing on the platform can't help but feel that the old station is ready and waiting for the next train and the distinguished resort guests that it's certain to bring. Amtrak's Cardinal train still stops at the station as it traverses West Virginia.

WHITE SULPHUR SPRINGS

For 30 years, The Greenbrier housed a top-secret bunker designed for the use of the U.S. Congress during a nuclear attack or other national emergency. Constructed between 1958 and 1961, the underground bunker was maintained in a constant state of readiness by a small cadre of government employees. Many Greenbrier employees knew about the bunker but willingly kept it secret. Exposed to the public in a news story published in The Washington Post in 1992, the U.S. Government Relocation Facility (as it officially was named) was soon phased out. Access to the massive facility—112,544 square feet on two levels—was protected by large steel and concrete doors such as this one. Today, the Greenbrier offers guided tours of the Cold War relic.

WHITE SULPHUR SPRINGS

Today, the village of White Sulphur Springs, located only minutes from the front entrance of the Greenbrier, lures visitors with its small-town charm and a variety of specialty shops and restaurants. These vintage hand-colored postcards show the village as it appeared around 1900 or so. The driver of the horse and buggy making its way down the dirt street soon would have to share the road with those new-fangled motorcars.

The Town of White Sulphur Springs, W. Va.

HOTEL HART, WHITE SULPHUR SPRINGS, W. VA. (2000 FT. ELEVATION)

Main Street, White Sulphur, W. Va.

Flash forward to the 1920s and you can see this trio of high-powered sedans parked outside the Hotel Hart, one of a number of White Sulphur places that over the years have welcomed travelers looking for a more affordable alternative to the fancy lodging at The Greenbrier.

Perhaps some of the Hotel Hart's guests took in a show at White Sulphur's Plaza Theater. Now demolished, the theater offered a variety of entertainment over the years.

THE PLAZA THEATRE, WHITE SULPHUR SPRINGS, W. VA.

Long a White Sulphur Springs landmark, this classic diner now has a new owner and a new name, but the same seven bar stools it's had since it first opened in the 1950s. It was long a popular breakfast spot for the late golfing great Sam Snead before he headed for the links each morning

Antique lovers have a variety of shops to choose from on White Sulphur's Main Street.

The late Russell Wease started out as a busboy at The Greenbrier and worked his way up in the ranks to become manager of the resort's popular Old White Lounge. He saved the money he received in tips and in the early 1950s was able to realize his long-time dream when he opened the Old White Inn in White Sulphur. Today the 26-room motel remains a popular stopover for both business and pleasure travelers.

White Sulphur's James Wylie House, now a bed and breakfast, was built in 1819 for pioneer Greenbrier County settler Richard Dixon as the centerpiece of his 1,300-acre farm. Fully restored, the house continues its long history of hosting weary travelers.

Opened in 1900, the White Sulphur Springs National Fish Hatchery is one of 65 federally owned fish hatcheries in the United States but one of only three producing Rainbow Trout. It produces 10 million trout eggs a year. The eggs are then shipped nationwide to federal, state and tribal hatcheries.

Here's a vintage postcard view of the National Fish Hatchery when it first opened in 1900.

The National Fish Hatchery is open to the public for guided and self-guided tours Monday through Friday from Memorial Day through Thanksgiving. The visitors center offers exhibits, aquariums and a display pool. A small amphitheater provides a setting for outdoor programs.

Established in 1884, Oakhurst Links, located just outside White Sulphur, is said to have been the first golf course organized in the United States. Golfers on the course must step back in time and use replica 1800s hickory clubs and gutta percha balls, precursors to today's rubber-core golf balls. No golf carts were available in the 1880s and so no carts are available today. Players must walk the course just like the early golfers.

Adding to the authenticity of the 19th Century golfing experience at Oakhurst Links is the flock of sheep that roams the course, keeping the fairways "mowed."

ORGAN CAVE

  Located on Route 63, south of the Midland Trail/U.S. 60, Organ Cave has about 40 miles of surveyed passages, making it one of the largest caves in West Virginia. The cave's name comes from a large calcite drapery that indeed resembles a pipe organ. As early as the 1820s, guests staying at the area's various sulphur spring resorts visited the cave. In the War of 1812 and again during the Civil War, the cave was mined for saltpeter to manufacture gunpowder. A 1932 newspaper photo showed two men examining some of the wooden hoppers used in the mining, secretly performed by the Confederate Army while Union troops unknowingly camped nearby. Today's visitors to the cave can still view the hoppers.

Saltpetre Hoppers in Organ Cave, W. Va.   Used by The Southern Confederacy
During Civil War

LEWISBURG

Lewisburg is located just a few minutes drive along the Midland Trail/U.S. 60 from The Greenbrier and White Sulphur Springs.

Midland Trail, Route U. S. 60 between White Sulphur Springs and Lewisburg, W. Va.

The seat of Greenbrier County and a regional trading center for the rolling countryside known as the Big Levels, Lewisburg has retained much of the appearance and charm of a quiet village of the Old South. This vintage postcard showing the Midland Trail through the town dates from the 1920s.

Midland Trail U. S. No. 60 through Lewisburg. W. Va.

GEN. ANDREW LEWIS

GENERAL ANDREW LEWIS SURVEYED
IN THIS VALLEY IN 1751 AND PROMOTED
SETTLEMENT. IN SEPTEMBER, 1774, HE
ORGANIZED HIS ARMY HERE AT CAMP
UNION, AND MARCHED TO POINT PLEASANT,
WHERE HE DEFEATED THE INDIANS UNDER
CORNSTALK IN THE FIRST BATTLE OF
THE REVOLUTION. FOR THE LEWISES THIS
TOWN WAS NAMED.

The town is named for Andrew Lewis. Born in Ireland in 1720, Lewis moved to Virginia with his parents in 1729. In 1751, he came to the Greenbrier area as a surveyor for the Greenbrier Land Company. He discovered a spring behind where the county courthouse now stands. The spring became known as Lewis' Spring. At the direction of General Braddock, Lewis built a crude fort, Fort Savannah, in 1755. The idea was to protect the settlers from Indian attack, but with the outbreak of the French and Indian War there were few settlers to protect. In 1774 the Royal Governor of Virginia, Lord Dunmore, ordered Lewis to assemble a militia force for an expedition against the united Shawnee, Delaware, Mingo and Ottawa tribes under Chief Cornstalk. Lewis assembled the army on the Big Levels, now Lewisburg, naming the assembly area Fort Union. After an arduous march of 161 miles, along what would become known as the Lewis Trail, the Virginia militia met and defeated the Indians at the battle of Point Pleasant on the Ohio River. Some have described the battle as the first of the American Revolution, but most historians scoff at that claim.

Today's downtown Lewisburg offers a comfortable mix of the past and present. Many 18th and 19th Century buildings remain, tastefully updated and put to new uses as shops, offices and restaurants. In 1978, a 236-acre area in the heart of Lewisburg was designated an historic district on the National Register of Historic Places. From the downtown radiates a network of wooded streets lined with sturdy homes of brick, frame or local limestone. Many of the homes have been in the same family for generations. (Photo courtesy the Greenbrier County Convention and Visitors Bureau.)

PORTFOLIO:
The General Lewis Hotel

One of the many fine homes built in Lewisburg in the early 1800s was the Withrow House, constructed in 1834 on Main Street at the eastern end of town. Flash forward to the 1920s when a young couple, Randolph K. and Mary Milton Hock moved to Lewisburg with the idea of taking the old Withrow House and, with additions, creating a new hotel celebrating the talents, handicrafts, and style of the early settlers. In May of 1929, the General Lewis Hotel opened.

Guests at today's General Lewis Inn can take their place in history as they register at the hand-built walnut and pine front desk, located just inside the popular inn's front door. The desk dates to 1760. Patrick Henry and Thomas Jefferson stood at this desk when they registered at the Sweet Chalybeate Springs Hotel, one of the area's many mineral springs resorts that were visited by the antebellum aristocrats of the South.

The original Withrow House is the east wing of the General Lewis, housing the inn's popular restaurant on the first floor and three guest rooms upstairs.

The General Lewis is furnished with authentic Colonial furniture. Randolph Hock spent years tracking down and acquiring spool and poster beds, bright coverlets and quilts, chests of drawers, collections of glass and china, old prints, corner cupboards and many other items that add to the inn's charm. Most of the items came from old homes in the Lewisburg area.

If the weather is right, guests at the General Lewis can enjoy a few minutes relaxing—and perhaps napping—in one of the comfortable rockers on the inn's front porch.

HISTORIC HOTEL DESK
GENERAL LEWIS HOTEL
Lewisburg West Virginia

WARMTH and CHEER
GENERAL LEWIS HOTEL
Lewisburg, West Virginia

DINING HALL
GENERAL LEWIS HOTEL
Lewisburg West Virginia

MASTER CHAMBER
GENERAL LEWIS HOTEL
Lewisburg West Virginia

"WEST VIEW" SLEEPING CHAMBER
GENERAL LEWIS HOTEL
Lewisburg West Virginia

PORCH
Simplicity and Relaxation
GENERAL LEWIS HOTEL
Lewisburg, W. Va.

OLD SWEET SPRINGS

Lewisburg's Carnegie Hall was built in 1902 with $33,000 donated by steel baron and philanthropist Andrew Carnegie to the former Lewisburg Female Institute, later the Greenbrier College for Women. After the college closed, Carnegie Hall Inc. was incorporated in 1983 as a regional not-for-profit arts and education center. Today the former classroom building is a cultural center that annually serves more than 75,000 patrons with live performances by artists

from around the world, arts in education programming, classes, workshops, fine art exhibits, an independent film series and more. The historic Greek-revival structure is one of only four Carnegie Halls still in continuous use in the world.

Greenbrier Military School was founded by Thomas Gilmore in 1890 as an academy for boys and became a military school in 1891. Known as the Lee Military Academy from 1896 until 1899, it offered college preparatory courses under "ideal" conditions, advertising that there was "no saloon in town; no distractions." In 1906, the Presbyterian Church purchased the academy and again conducted it as a school for boys until 1920, when it became a privately owned military school.

This undated postcard shows cadets assembling on the parade ground.

Aerial View of Greenbrier Military School   Lewisburg, West Virginia

The Greenbrier Military School closed in 1972 and its buildings on Lee Street were acquired for the newly opened West Virginia School of Osteopathic Medicine.

Built in 1820, the North House Museum, 301 West Washington Street in Lewisburg, contains the collections of the Greenbrier Historical Society, including many of the finest examples of early Virginia furnishings. The museum, shown here in a snow-covered scene, is open Mondays through Saturday, from 10 a.m. to 4 p.m. (Photo courtesy the Greenbrier Historical Society.)

The inscription on the base of the Confederate Monument in Lewisburg reads "In Memory of Our Confederate Dead." The Confederate Cemetery on the edge of downtown Lewisburg is the final resting place of 95 soldiers killed in the Battle of Lewisburg on May 23, 1862, and the nearby Battle of Droop Mountain on November 6, 1863.

CONFEDERATE MONUMENT   LEWISBURG, W. VA.

Greenbrier County Court House, Lewisburg, W. Va.

2500 Feet above Sea Level

When the Virginia General Assembly incorporated Lewisburg as a town in 1782, the first courthouse was a temporary log structure. A permanent courthouse was built on Market Street in 1837 and has been in continuous use ever since. The building's original section was fashioned from locally made brick. While the exterior appearance of the red brick structure has changed very little over the years, extensive interior alternations have been made. And two wings have been added—the first in 1937 and the second in 1963.

Lewisburg's Old Stone Church at Church and Foster streets is the oldest church in continuous use west of the Allegheny Mountains. The original congregation was established in 1783 and the current building was constructed in 1796. It's built of limestone blocks that are said to have been brought on horseback by the women of the church, from the banks of the Greenbrier River four miles away. The interior of the Old Stone church has been rearranged, but the original pews, balcony (where slaves sat) and pulpit remain. During the Civil War the church was used as a military hospital and later for billeting troops. Today, the church serves the Presbyterian Congregation of Lewisburg and the builders' original inscription is still in place over the church doorway.

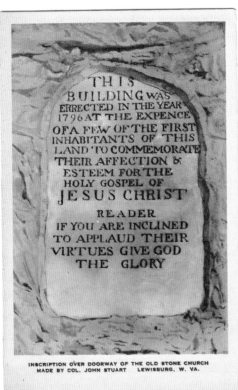

INSCRIPTION OVER DOORWAY OF THE OLD STONE CHURCH
MADE BY COL. JOHN STUART   LEWISBURG, W. VA.

WEST VIRGINIA STATE FAIR

As early as the 1880s, a West Virginia State Fair was held in Wheeling. But in 1941 the Legislature declared the annual fair held each August at Fairlea, just a short drive south from Lewisburg on U.S. 219, to be the official West Virginia State Fair. It includes competitive exhibitions by farmers and 4H and FFA members, exhibitions by manufacturers of farm equipment, concerts by musical performers, a beauty pageant, a traveling carnival and harness races such as this one, long one of the fair's most popular events.

Racing at the West Virginia State Fair at Lewisburg

In the rural America of yesteryear, when farmers farmed with horses, it wasn't unusual for a farmer to tell his neighbor: "Hey, I bet my horse can pull more than yours can." Then to prove it, the neighbor would take him up on that bet and soon a competition would be in full swing. Today's modern-day equivalents are organized draft horse pulling contests such as this one at the West Virginia State Fair.

In 1938 *Life* magazine featured the West Virginia State Fair on its cover and in a photo essay within the publication. Prior to the completion of Interstate 64 in 1988, the fairground was difficult to access from most of the state and the event was much more local in nature. However, it has grown greatly since that time. The fair has attracted over 35,000 people on big days. It's estimated that the fair has an annual economic impact of $8.9 million on Greenbrier County.

RONCEVERTE

C. & O R. R. Station.   Ronceverte, W. Va.

Continuing south on U.S. 219 brings one to the charming little town of Ronceverte. First settled circa 1775, the community was a sleepy little place of a half-dozen houses and a gristmill until the arrival of the Chesapeake & Ohio Railway in 1872. Virtually overnight, it exploded into a noisy railroad town where the whistle of steam locomotives mixed with the scream of band-saws cutting lumber from logs floated down the Greenbrier River from great white pine forests along its tributaries. It was the mill's owner, Cecil Clay, who gave the town its name when it was incorporated in 1882. The name is a French word meaning "greenbrier." Clay said he saw the name on an old map and simply liked the sound of it. In 1915, the C&O built this stately craftsman style train station in the heart of town. As of this writing, the station is still standing.

MOUNTAIN MEADOW

The Midland Trail/U.S. 60 west of Lewisburg follows the route of the Meadow River for several miles in western Greenbrier County and crosses Meadow Mountain at an altitude of 2,710 feet above sea level. The Meadow is a major tributary of the Gauley River.

Meadow Mountain west of Lewisburg, West Va. on U. S. Route 60

CLINTONVILLE

Clintonville is an unincorporated community along U.S. 60 in western Greenbrier County. "George and I are on our way to White Sulphur Springs" was the message written on the back of this Clintonville postcard, mailed in 1931.

SAM BLACK CHURCH

Sam Black Church is located on the Midland Trail/U.S. 60 at its Greenbrier County junction with Interstate 64. A small bell tower rises above the hipped roof of the picturesque white frame structure. The church was erected in 1902 in memory of the Rev. Sam Black, an early Southern Methodist circuit rider. On his horse, Shiloh, Black traveled the back roads of a half dozen West Virginia counties, organizing congregations and building churches with the money he obtained from selling socks, gloves and other handmade items made by the women of the church.

Sam Black Church is also known for the tale of the Greenbrier Ghost. The death of Zona Heaster Shue in 1897 was presumed natural until her spirit appeared to her mother to tell her that her husband Edward had killed her. She said he had attacked her in a fit of rage and had broken her neck. To prove this, the ghost turned her head completely around until it was facing backwards. An autopsy on the exhumed body verified the apparition's account. Her neck had been broken and her windpipe crushed. Edward, found guilty of murder, was sentenced to the West Virginia State Penitentiary at Moundsville, where he died three years later. As this roadside marker attests, this is the only known case where a culprit was convicted on the testimony of a ghost.

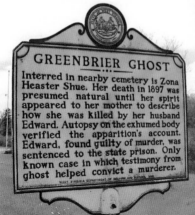

GREENBRIER GHOST

Interred in nearby cemetery is Zona Heaster Shue. Her death in 1897 was presumed natural until her spirit appeared to her mother to describe how she was killed by her husband Edward. Autopsy on the exhumed body verified the apparition's account. Edward, found guilty of murder, was sentenced to the state prison. Only known case in which testimony from ghost helped convict a murderer.

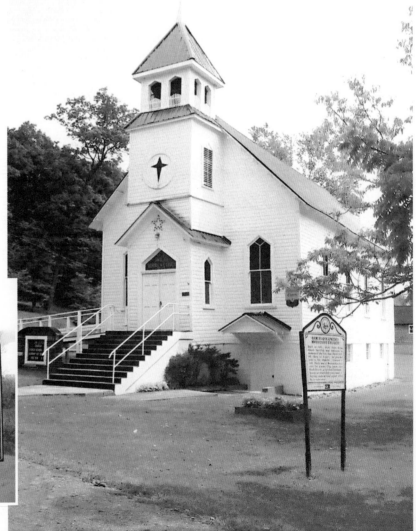

34

RUPERT

The first settlers in the area now known as Rupert called it Big Clear Creek. A post office opened under that name in 1851, but later was discontinued. In 1867, the post office was re-established with Cyrus A. Rupert as postmaster. Rupert was the region's first doctor, a lawyer and general store owner. Legend has it that the town was having difficulty getting mail because there were too many post offices in West Virginia named Clear Creek, so in 1888 the name was changed to Rupert. Here's a view of the neatly kept Mt. Rupert United Methodist Church, on Route 33 just off the Midland Trail/U.S. 60 and about 30 miles west of White Sulphur.

BLACK'S TOURIST COURT
Rupert, W. Va.   U. S. Route 60

Before Memphis entrepreneur Kemmons Wilson built his first Holiday Inn in 1952 and revolutionized the lodging industry with what he called "inexpensive luxury," travelers had to make do with roadside establishments that offered less-than-luxurious cabins. This postcard from Black's Tourist Court in Rupert boasted that it had "Private Baths, Toilet (and) Steam Heated Cabins," and served plate lunches.

RAINELLE

Around 1906, brothers John and W.T. Raine, for whom the town of Rainelle is named, established the Meadow River Lumber Company, which became one of the largest hardwood plants in the eastern United States, employing 500 men. *The West Virginia Encyclopedia* (2006) describes Rainelle as "a model company town with public water, electricity, and nice houses with yards and garden plots." This antique photo suggests the community was a thriving place.

According to *West Virginia, A Guide to the Mountain State* (1941), the triple band-saws at the Meadow River Lumber Company could cut some 35 million feet of lumber annually, or five carloads daily. Logs were transported to the mill twice daily by rail from the upper Meadow River Valley. In the lumberyard, lumber was stacked to a height of 20 or 30 feet. After the stacked lumber was thoroughly seasoned, it was put through the finishing mill, where it is smoothed and converted into building materials, furniture stock, or flooring. One of the specialty products produced at the plant was wooden heels for women's shoes. It turned out more than four million heels a year.

In 1970, the Meadow River Lumber Company was sold to Georgia-Pacific. In 1975, Georgia-Pacific tore down the old, outdated mill and built a modern mill in a new location. This photograph shows a portion of the abandoned mill shortly before it was demolished. The original mill site is now a shopping center.

The King Coal Hotel in East Rainelle was a busy place back in the day when coal was king. Not visible in this photograph is something the hotel was famous for: a three-ton lump of coal that stood outside.

King Coal Hotel
East Rainelle, West Va.

FAYETTE COUNTY

Continuing its course to the west, the Midland Trail/U.S. 60 leaves Greenbrier County and heads into Fayette County.

Fayette County was created by Act of the Virginia General Assembly, passed February 28, 1831, from parts of Greenbrier, Kanawha, Nicholas and Logan counties. It was named in honor of the Marquis de Lafayette, who had played a key role in assisting the Continental Army during the American Revolution. A substantial portion was subdivided from Fayette County to form Raleigh County in 1850. Fayette was one of 50 counties that broke off from the rest of Virginia and formed the new state of West Virginia in 1863 at the height of the Civil War.

The county consists of a high plateau bordered on the east by Sewell Mountain and on the west by the Kanawha Valley. The New River carves the spectacular New River Gorge across the county from north to south, effectively dividing it into eastern and western halves.

EASTERN FAYETTE COUNTY

Sewell Mountain, located in Greenbrier and Fayette counties, is one of the highest mountains in southern West Virginia and at 3,180 feet is the highest point on the Midland Trail. The mountain and the nearby town of Sewell take their name from reclusive pioneer Stephen Sewell. It's thought that Sewell was killed by nearby Indians in the late 1700s, though his remains were never found. He first settled with Jacob Marlin near present day Marlinton, West Virginia, when the region was still a wilderness.

VIEW OF SEWELL MOUNTAIN (ELEVATION 3,180 FEET), ON MIDLAND, TRAIL, NEAR CHARLESTON, W. VA.

Today's U.S. 60 traces the original course of the earlier Midland Trail and James River & Kanawha Turnpike as it crosses Sewell Mountain west of Rainelle at an upland pass near Myles Knoll at Maywood. Its course across the mountain is winding and subject to heavy winter snows.

The caption on this vintage postcard, postmarked in 1934, shows the summit of Sewell Mountain on the Midland Trail and describes it as "near Charleston, W.Va.," although in fact Charleston lies roughly 50 miles to the west.

In 1861, Union and Confederate forces both bivouacked on Sewell Mountain, though no battle erupted there. It was here that General Robert E. Lee first saw his treasured horse, Traveler, that he later purchased for $200 in Confederate currency. On the Midland Trail/U.S. 60 a bit more than two miles west of the Greenbrier County line, Cavendish Road leads travelers to a fenced tree and rock that mark the spot where Lee pitched his headquarters tent and first glimpsed Traveler.

BABCOCK STATE PARK

At the Midland Trail/U.S. 60 intersection with Route 41 is the entrance to Babcock State Park. The park offers its visitors 4,127 acres of serene yet rugged beauty, a fast-flowing trout stream in a boulder-strewn canyon and mountain vistas to be viewed from several scenic overlooks.

Scene in Babcock State Park, on Route U. S. 60, West Virginia   28-H647

Babcock Park, which opened in 1937, was built as a Depression-era public works project, with the main facilities and trails constructed by the young workers of the Civilian Conservation Corps (CCC). The park headquarters, 12 cabins, a stable, superintendent's house, a natural swimming pool and picnic facilities were constructed from locally quarried stone and logs from American chestnut trees that had fallen victim to the chestnut blight. CCC workers hand-forged door latches and other metalwork on the site. Additional facilities built in the 1970s include a modern in-ground swimming pool made necessary because acid mine drainage from nearby strip mining had degraded the water quality of Glade Creek, making it no longer suitable as a source for the natural swimming pool shown here.

Swimming Pool and Administration Building, Babcock State Park, W. Va.   9A-H2446

The Glade Creek Grist Mill, surely one of the most photographed sites in West Virginia, may look old but was actually constructed in 1976. A working mill, it was assembled from parts of three other West Virginia mills that were dismantled and moved piece by piece to Babcock. Grinding grain by a rushing stream was once a way of life in West Virginia. It's estimated that the state once had as many as 500 similar mills. Today, nearly all are gone—victims of "progress."

CAMP WASHINGTON CARVER

At Clifftop, also on Route 41, is Camp Washington Carver. Named to jointly honor black leaders Booker T. Washington and George Washington Carver, it was the country's first 4-H camp for African Americans. In 1942, the Works Progress Administration and the Civilian Conservation Corps built the park's great chestnut lodge, the largest log structure in West Virginia. Today, the camp operates as a rural cultural center, hosting a number of events each summer. The weeklong Appalachian String Band Music Festival attracts thousands of music lovers to the camp each August.

SPY ROCK

Located on the old James River & Kanawha Turnpike about 18 miles east of Hawks Nest and about midway between Charleston and Lewisburg, Spy Rock is a large rock ledge that provided an ideal lookout along the turnpike. In the early 19th Century, both Indians and whites used the rock as a vantage point. During the Civil War, Union and Confederate troops alike used it to monitor enemy troop movements along the Midland Trail.

HICO

At Hico, five miles east of Ansted, the Midland Trail/U.S. 60 intersects with Route 19, an important gateway to Interstates 79 and 77. Travelers who head south can see the famed New River Gorge Bridge, one of the world's longest single-span steel arch bridges, can enjoy white-water rafting and other recreational offerings on the New River Gorge National River and visit the historic town of Fayetteville. To the north, there's rafting on the Gauley River, the Summersville Dam and Lake and Carnifex Ferry Battlefield State Park.

A familiar spot for yesterday's travelers on the Midland Trail/U.S. 60 was the Shady Oaks Tourist Camp, which welcomed folks in the era before the advent of modern motels.

Shady Oaks Tourist Camp On U. S. 60 Hico, W. Va.

31981

ANSTED AND HAWKS NEST

Ansted was first named New Haven by a company of spiritualists who arrived from New England in 1830, but the following year, when the town became the county seat for Fayette County, it was renamed Ansted for Professor David T. Ansted, a British scientist who was instrumental in interesting English capitalists in the development of the region's coal seams.

This view from the top of Gauley Mountain looks over the town of Ansted (at lower left) toward the New River Gorge and its soaring bridge, nearly six miles away.

Ansted's growth dates from 1873 when the arrival of the C&O Railway opened up coal operations nearby. On a knoll in the middle of town, the renovated mansion of mining engineer, coal operator and railroad builder William Nelson Page still stands as evidence of the once thriving coal business. From 1889 to 1917, Page was president of Gauley Mountain Coal Co. in Ansted. He also played a key role in development of the Virginian Railway. When Page retired and moved to Washington, D.C., the house stood empty for several years. Captain John Vawter, who managed the company store in Ansted, then occupied it. Locally, the house is known as the Page-Vawter House. This photograph shows the historic house before a recent restoration effort got underway.

In Westlake Cemetery, which covers the crest of a small knoll overlooking the main part of Ansted, is the grave of Julia Neale Jackson, the mother of Confederate General Stonewall Jackson. In 1855, then-Major Jackson visited the grave and noted in a letter to an aunt that it was unmarked. After the Civil War ended, Captain Thomas Ranson, a veteran of the Stonewall Brigade and a great admirer of Jackson, erected a marble monument at the site.

THE GRAVE OF STONEWALL JACKSON'S MOTHER AT ANSTEAD, W. VA.

This antique postcard shows the grave of Julia Neale Jackson as it appeared before installation of the iron fence that now encloses it.

Halfway House in the east end of Ansted was so named because it stood halfway between Lewisburg and Charleston on the James River & Kanawha Turnpike and was a popular stopover for turnpike travelers. It's thought to be the oldest structure in Fayette County. The original building dated from before the American Revolution. William Tyree rebuilt it in 1810. Among the tavern's many famous guests were Daniel Webster and Henry Clay. During the Civil War it was used by both Union and Confederate troops. The tavern closed in 1927, and since then the structure has been used as a private home.

HAWKS NEST STATE PARK

Hawks Nest, the site of Hawks Nest State Park, is a peak on Gauley Mountain in Ansted, overlooking the New River Gorge. The cliffs at this point rise 585 feet above the New River, providing a breathtaking view of the river and the wooded hillsides below. Chief Justice of the United States John Marshall visited the area in 1812 and for a short time thereafter it was known as Marshall's Pillar. When the James River & Kanawha Turnpike was constructed in the 1820s, the rocky formation overlooking the gorge became a popular stopping place for travelers. The name Hawks Nest derived from the many hawks that previously inhabited the massive cliffs. When the C&O Railway arrived and began blasting a path for its tracks, the hawks left and never returned. C&O work crews laid two sections of track. One section started in Richmond, Virginia, and worked its way west. The other began in Huntington and headed east. The two sections met at Hawks Nest on January 29, 1873.

VIEW NEAR HAWKS
NEST ROCK ROUTE
#60

In 1930, the Hawks Nest Rock Resort, a private venture, operated on top of the mountain. A brochure issued by the resort indicated it had a public dining room (open from April through September), a five-room rental cottage, an observation tower and "a menagerie of reasonable proportions." The brochure included this photograph of the Midland Trail/U.S. 60. Note the absence of a centerline on the narrow roadway.

The Hawks Nest Dam was constructed in the 1930s to provide water for a hydroelectric station built to generate power for an electro-metallurgical plant at the town of Alloy, downstream on the Kanawha River. The construction of a tunnel to divert the waters of the New River through Gauley Mountain as part of the project resulted in West Virginia's worst industrial disaster. With jobs scarce in Depression-era West Virginia, workers—mostly African Americans and poor whites—flocked to the project. Many paid a high price for the meager wages they earned. They died from breathing the silica rock dust that was stirred up by the digging. Many of the victims were buried in secret. The company digging the tunnel acknowledged 109 deaths, but a subsequent congressional hearing placed the actual death toll at nearly 500. Some who have researched the tragedy believe the actual death toll may have been far higher.

Following completion of the dam in 1934, the state bought the surrounding land for use as a state park. The Civilian Conservation Corps erected an attractive group of stone, log and frame structures for the use of park visitors, including this snack and souvenir shop, a picnic shelter and a scenic overlook.

An oddity in the original park construction was an unusual two-story stone restroom, uniquely shaped like the round tower of a medieval castle. It can be seen at the right of this vintage postcard. That's the Midland Trail/U.S. 60 running through the center of the card. The parking lot on the far side of the road seems full. The photo for the card must have been taken at the height of the summer vacation season.

Just below the lodge at Hawks Nest State Park, fabled Lovers Leap Rock juts out over the New River Gorge. It was there that, according to legend, a Cherokee maiden and a Shawnee brave jumped to their deaths because their parents opposed their marriage. Or maybe it was an Indian maiden and a young white settler who leaped to the deaths. Then again, perhaps it was a boy and girl from feuding pioneer families. Chose any variation of the oft-told tale you please. This much is certain: The outcropping of rock provides an impressive view but the path getting there is not for the faint of heart.

PORTFOLIO:
A Visit to Hawks Nest

Hawks Nest State Park has been attracting fun-seekers, both West Virginians and out-of-state travelers alike, for more than 70 years. The park's scenic overlook provides a view of the river below that's truly awe-inspiring.

The park's Depression-era buildings are located on the north side of the Midland Trail/U.S. 60. In 1967, the state built a new lodge on the south side of the highway about a half-mile east of the original complex.

Starkly modern in design, the new lodge was designed by The Architects Collaborative (TAC), a Boston firm founded by famed architect Walter Gropius. The design of the lodge, much like a modern hotel, provides a sharp contrast with the earlier structures but guests clearly enjoy the air conditioning, cable television and a dining room with oversized windows to better take in the spectacular views.

In recent years, the park has added an aerial tram that takes visitors down to the river level, 600 feet below, where they can board a jetboat for a spin on the river.

THE MYSTERY HOLE

Located just two minutes from Hawks Nest State Park, the Mystery Hole is hard to miss. It's the only building you're going to see that has a Volkswagen Beetle sticking out of its side. The Mystery Hole long has been a quirky favorite of Midland Trail/U.S. 60 travelers. It's hard to describe what visitors experience during the brief guided tour. The usual laws of Nature—things like the law of gravity—don't seem to apply to the Mystery Hole. Some cynical souls scoff and call it a "tourist trap." Other visitors leave with bewildered looks on their faces and say their visit was as close to the Twilight Zone as they care to get.

CHIMNEY CORNER

Driving the Midland Trail/U.S. 60 across Gauley Mountain between Hawks Nest and Gauley Bridge can be a challenge, especially for those drivers not accustomed to a two-lane asphalt highway that refuses to follow a straight line, instead constantly twisting and turning and climbing up and down. But the drive has its scenic rewards, such as that at Chimney Corner.

View of Chimney Corner, Junction of Midland Trail near Gauley Bridge, W. Va. — D-37

This stopover in the unincorporated town of Chimney Corner, located at the intersection of the Midland Trail/U.S. 60 and Route 16, has been attracting tourists and locals alike since 1928. In the years since, it's been everything from a speakeasy, beer joint, gas station and restaurant to the charming stopover it is today. The Ole Country Store specializes in hand-made crafts, old-time candies and sodas and offers an appealing front porch where you just might want to sit a spell. Don't doze off! (Photo courtesy the Chimney Corner Ole Country Store.)

GAULEY BRIDGE

The town of Gauley Bridge hugs a steep corner of mountainous real estate above the point where the New and Gauley rivers join to form the Kanawha River. History tells us a fellow named Miller operated a ferry and tavern here until a toll bridge was built on the then-new James River & Kanawha Turnpike in 1822. The bridge stood for about four years, until a fire attributed to "persons interested in the ferry" destroyed it.

View of Gauley Bridge, W. Va. on U. S. 60, Showing Junction of Gauley and New Rivers

A second bridge was built in 1848—and burned by the retreating Confederate Army in 1861. The old Miller Tavern became a headquarters for the Union Army. Among the officers stationed there were William McKinley and Rutherford B. Hayes, both destined for the presidency of the United States.

The crumbling stone piers of the second bridge at Gauley Bridge, the one burned by the retreating Confederate Army, can still be seen in the river. The bridge next to it is a railroad span. Today's highway bridge is not visible in this old postcard view.

PIERS OF BRIDGE DESTROYED DURING CIVIL WAR, GAULEY BRIDGE, W.VA.

GLEN FERRIS

The community of Glen Ferris was known until 1895 as Stockton, for Colonel Andrew Stockton, who settled in the area in 1812. During the early days of the James River & Kanawha Turnpike, Stockton kept a popular tavern where travelers could get food, drink and a bed for the night. The genial host, a prosperous salt entrepreneur and gentleman farmer, was described by one of his patrons as "a good-natured chunk of a man who cast a shadow of almost the small altitude when lying down as when standing up."

The last stagecoach rolled along the turnpike in 1873, robbed of passengers by the newly arrived Chesapeake & Ohio Railway. But even so, Stockton's tavern survived and in 1929 was converted into the popular Glen Ferris Inn.

KANAWHA FALLS, W. VA.   ON C. & O. R. R.

KANAWHA FALLS

From the Glen Ferris Inn is a fine view of Kanawha Falls, extending in a jagged line across the river, with a drop of 22 feet. A small dam has been built above the falls to generate power. The waters slip smoothly over the lip of the dam in a swirling confusion of white foam. A crag overlooking the falls is known as Van Biber Leap, named for Ruben Van Biber, a pioneer, who is said to have jumped into the river and successfully escaped a band of pursuing Indians.

A huge rock overhangs a back road near Kanawha Falls. Look closely and you'll see a driver piloting an open automobile under the rock. The railroad tracks visible behind the car belong to the long-gone Kanawha & Michigan Railroad that once ran from Ohio to Gauley Bridge by way of Point Pleasant and Charleston.

HANGING ROCK, NEAR KANAWHA FALLS, W. VA., ON K. & M. R. R.

ALLOY and BOOMER

The tunnel project at Hawks Nest that claimed so many lives was built to supply power to a Union Carbide Corp. electro-metallurgical plant at the unincorporated community of Alloy located along the Kanawha River and the Midland Trail/U.S. 60 about five miles west of Gauley Bridge. Alloy was originally known as Boncar (that's "Carbon" spelled backwards). Both the original name and the current name refer to the silicon alloys plant that still operates at Alloy. Union Carbide sold the plant to a Norwegian company, Elkem, in 1981. Elkem then sold it to Globe Metallurgical Inc. in 2005. Silicon goes into a long list of products, including computer chips. It's been estimated that half of the world's computers contains chips with silicon refined at Alloy. The plant once employed as many as 2,000 workers. Its current workforce numbers about 250.

The town of Boomer, on the Midland Trail/U.S. 60 just west of Alloy, grew up around the coal industry. A thick seam of coal running through the hills above the town attracted mining operations as early as 1896, and the arrival of the Kanawha & Michigan Railroad provided a means of shipping that coal to market. The Boomer Coal and & Coke operations recruited Italian immigrants to work in the mines, and that Italian heritage can still be seen in the town's brightly colored hillside homes that originated as company houses.

SMITHERS and MONTGOMERY

The history of Smithers is closely intertwined with the Midland Trail. Around 1825, the James River & Kanawha Turnpike was completed through Smithers west to Charleston. One of the region's earliest settlers was James Smithers, for whom the town is named.

Travelers on the Midland Trail/U.S. 60 can visit Montgomery, nestled on the southern bank of the Kanawha River, by crossing the river via the Earle M. Vickers Memorial Bridge. Vickers was the grandson of town founder James C. Montgomery. A three-term member of the West Virginia House of Delegates, Vickers became director of the state Office of Legislative Services and held that post until his retirement in 1993. He died in 2001.

Nestled on the southern bank of the Kanawha River, Montgomery is located in both Fayette and Kanawha County. First known as Coal Valley, it was incorporated in 1891 and named for founder James Montgomery, a gentleman farmer with extensive business interests in the region.

Aerial View of Montgomery, W. Va. on the Kanawha River showing buildings of West Virginia Institute of Technology, C & O Railway and Route 60

Montgomery soon became the commercial center for the surrounding coal mining and ferro-alloy industries. This vintage postcard showing the town's Railroad Avenue dates from the early 1900s. Business signs that can be seen along the avenue include the Central Hotel, the Weaver Drug Co., the Davis Department Store and the Mecca Saloon—all of them no doubt busy places in the young town.

A GLIMPSE OF FRONT, NEW RIVER STATE SCHOOL, MONTGOMERY, W. VA.

An important factor in Montgomery's growth over the years has been the presence of what today is known as the West Virginia University Institute of Technology and Technical College, or "Institute" for short. Its history dates back more than 100 years, to the founding of Montgomery Preparatory School in 1895. Various changes in name and mission followed over the years.

By 1921, it was known as the New River Trade School. In 1931, it became New River State College and in 1941 was renamed West Virginia Institute of Technology. In 1996, the college became WVU's largest regional campus. Old Main, shown above in a vintage postcard, still serves the Institute campus.

C. & O. STATION, MONTGOMERY, W. VA.

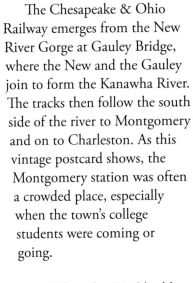

The Chesapeake & Ohio Railway emerges from the New River Gorge at Gauley Bridge, where the New and the Gauley join to form the Kanawha River. The tracks then follow the south side of the river to Montgomery and on to Charleston. As this vintage postcard shows, the Montgomery station was often a crowded place, especially when the town's college students were coming or going.

C. & O. R. R. STATION, MONTGOMERY, W. VA.

When the C&O's old frame station began showing its age, the railroad replaced it with this handsome brick structure. Compared with the earlier postcard, it seems almost deserted. But the Montgomery station remained busy right up to the end of rail passenger service in 1971. The stone building behind the station at the right of the card is the former Merchants National Bank.

In 2010, members of the WVU Creative Design Team created this bright new mural on the side of the Modern Barbershop on Montgomery's Third Avenue. The mural features a train, downtown buildings and, in the background, the Vickers Memorial Bridge. (Photo courtesy the Charleston *Daily Mail*.)

KANAWHA COUNTY

Kanawha County, named for the Kanawha River that runs through it, was created November 14, 1788. Originally, the county was 10 times its present size but was greatly decreased in size as other counties were carved from it. Even so, it remains West Virginia's fourth largest county. Charleston is both the county seat and the capital of West Virginia.

The salt industry stimulated the county's early economic development. Fifty-two furnaces were producing 3,000 bushels of salt per day by 1815, and three times that number by the late 1840s. Originally, the furnaces were fueled by wood, but as timber grew scarce coal soon became the fuel of choice.

LONDON

LOCK AND DAM ON KANAWHA RIVER, AT LONDON, W. VA.

The U.S. Army Corps of Engineers began construction of dams on the Kanawha in the late 1880s, building 10 dams of French design. When completed in 1898, they provided year-round commercial navigation on the Kanawha for 90 miles, from Boomer downstream to Point Pleasant, where the Kanawha flows into the Ohio. In the 1930s, the original dams were replaced with new high-lift dams at Winfield, Marmet and London. This vintage postcard shows the London Locks and Dam, located about two miles downstream from Montgomery, as it appeared shortly after its completion in 1934.

GLASGOW and CEDAR GROVE

The small Kanawha County community of Glasgow is located on a beautiful bend in the Kanawha and its history has always been closely tied to the river. Today, an American Electric Power generating plant at Glasgow burns more than a million tons of coal a year, all of it delivered by river barge. Local tradition says the name Glasgow comes from a combination of the word "glass" with the word "company" because the town was formerly home to a glass factory. But the presence of many Scottish immigrants in this region suggests the town might also have named after the Scottish city of Glasgow.

Cedar Grove is the oldest community in Kanawha County. It dates to 1773, some 14 years before the settlement of Fort Lee, Charleston's predecessor. The first settler was Walter Kelly, for whom Kelly's Creek is named. When Indians killed Kelly and his black servant, William Morris bought his land and moved his family there. Following the American Revolution, a steady flow of new families settled in the area. In 1790, the Old State Road was completed to Cedar Grove and it became a terminus for land travel and a beginning point for water traffic that could make its way down the Kanawha to the Ohio. Not surprisingly a boat building industry grew up. The dugout canoes used by Lewis & Clark for their famous westward expedition were crafted in Cedar Grove.

Virginia's Chapel in Cedar Grove—sometimes called "The Little Brick Church"—was built by salt industrialist William Tompkins in 1853 as a graduation present for his daughter Virginia, the eldest of the 10 Tompkins children. Both sides used the chapel as a hospital during the Civil War. It was deeded to the Upper Kanawha Valley Council in 1979 and restored in 1981.

BELLE

"The Old Stone House" in Belle was built sometime between 1800 and 1810 by Samuel Shrewsberry Sr., one of the pioneer settlers in the Kanawha Valley. The exterior walls are 18 inches thick and made of sandstone quarried from the nearby hills. The interior walls, cupboards and woodwork are of hand-hewn walnut. The house has been restored and is operated as a museum by the Belle Historical Restoration Society Inc.

Since it began production in 1926, the E. I. du Pont de Nemours & Co. Inc. plant at Belle has developed more than 120 chemical processes. The Belle facility was the nation's first commercial ammonia synthesis site. It was at Belle that DuPont developed the technology to manufacture nylon, and the Belle plant produced the nation's first synthetic urea for fertilizers and plastics.

MALDEN

Malden, originally called Terra Salis and later known as the Kanawha Salines, was the center of an extensive salt industry from roughly 1800 until the Civil War. Today, the little residential community is best known as the boyhood home of Booker T. Washington (1856-1915), who rose from slavery to become one of the nation's greatest black leaders.

As a newly freed slave, a nine-year-old Washington walked to Malden with his mother from the Virginia plantation that had been their home. At Malden, the family lived in this crude cabin. Young Washington worked at the salt furnaces and later in a coal mine. When a school for blacks was opened, he attended it by day and worked at night. He went on to graduate from Hampton Institute in Virginia, and then returned to Malden to teach before leaving West Virginia. In 1881, he established his own school at Tuskegee, Alabama, and built it into the premier black school of its day.

Malden is home to the African Zion Baptist Church, founded in 1852, where Washington taught Sunday school. A replica of his boyhood cabin has been erected behind the church. Tours of the church and cabin can be arranged by contacting the Booker T. Washington Institute at West Virginia State University.

Hale House in Malden was formerly owned by Dr. John P. Hale, a physician from Hales Ford, Virginia, who became one of the Kanawha Valley's most successful salt industrialists and coal entrepreneurs. In 1871, he was elected mayor of Charleston.

A physician named Richard E. Putney, who practiced medicine in the Malden area for over 50 years, built the Putney House in 1836. Today, the Putney House is used as a law office.

Charleston, West Virginia's largest city, is situated on the Kanawha River at the mouth of the Elk River. The first settlers arrived in 1788 and built what was known as Fort Lee near the present downtown. Their leader was George Clendenin, and in 1894 the Virginia General Assembly chartered a town known as Charlestown, named for Clendenin's father, Charleston. Later the name would be shortened to Charleston. The local salt industry helped to build Charleston's early economy. The James River & Kanawha Turnpike, linking the city with Virginia, arrived in the 1820s.

Daniel Boone (1734-1820) was born in Pennsylvania, lived briefly in North Carolina, died in Missouri and is most often associated with Kentucky, scene of many of his legendary exploits. But West Virginia, too, can lay claim to a piece of that legend. In the late 1780s and early 1790s the famous frontiersman lived in a cabin in Kanawha County. This vintage postcard—printed and distributed by Charleston's old Daniel Boone Hotel—shows a marker paying tribute to Boone. The marker, erected by the Kanawha Valley Chapter of the Daughters of the American Revolution, stands in Daniel Boone Park on the Midland Trail/U.S. 60 on the eastern outskirts of Charleston.

Daniel Boone Park also contains the Craik-Patton House and the Ruffner Log cabin.

James Craik and his wife, Juliet Shrewsbury, built the Greek Revival style Craik-Patton House in 1834. A relative of George Washington, Craik came to Charleston as a lawyer, but later studied for the ministry and was ordained. In 1846, he left Charleston to accept a call from a church in Louisville, Kentucky. George S. Patton and his family lived in the Craik-Patton House from 1858 until his death as a Colonel in the Confederate Army during the Civil War. General George S. Patton III, one of World War II's most famous military leaders, was the grandson of Colonel Patton. The Craik-Patton House originally stood on Virginia Street in downtown Charleston but was moved to Lee Street in 1906 when a new street cut through the original site. It was saved from destruction when it was acquired by the City of Charleston in 1965 and leased to the West Virginia chapter of the National Society of Colonial Dames in America, which moved it to its present site.

Like the Craik-Patton House, the Ruffner cabin wasn't originally situated in Daniel Boone Park. The log cabin originally stood at 1538 Kanawha Boulevard. Built in 1803 by Joseph Ruffner for his family on a property that used to be called Rosedale, the cabin is said to be one of the oldest extant houses in Kanawha County. The current cabin is actually a replica—the original Ruffner cabin was torn down in 1969.

In early Charleston, the municipal cemetery was a small plot next to the Kanawha River on the James River & Kanawha Turnpike. By 1869 the old burial ground had run out of space and so the city began Spring Hill Cemetery on a hill overlooking the town. A.J. Vosburg, a civil engineer, designed the cemetery's Old Circle section, which incorporated beautiful geometric patterns for the walkouts, typical of the Victorian Era.

A visually striking feature of Spring Hill is this large mausoleum built in 1910. With its stone façade and tile roof, the Moorish style architecture of the mausoleum is a striking contrast to the architecture typically seen in the region.

Morris Harvey College Buildings, Charleston, W. Va.

The University of Charleston campus stands on the south side of the Kanawha River, just across the river from the Capitol Complex and the Midland Trail/ U.S. 60. The school, known at that time as Morris Harvey College, moved to Charleston from its original home in Barboursville in 1935. At first it operated in temporary quarters but moved to its current location in 1947. This vintage postcard dates from the 1950s. Shown at the center of the card is the school's main administration and office classroom, built in 1950-51. Named Riggleman Hall, it honors Leonard Riggleman, the school's president from 1931 to 1964.

Renamed the University of Charleston in 1978, the school thrived in the 1990s under the stewardship of President Ed Welch. The Clay Tower Building, shown here, housing science labs, library and electronic classrooms was dedicated in 1997. The construction of new dormitories followed. A pharmacy school was opened in 2006 and graduated its first class in May 2010.

William Alexander MacCorkle (1857-1930) served as West Virginia governor from 1893 to 1897 and was elected to the U.S. Senate in 1910. Between those stints, he built his Sunrise mansion in Charleston's South Hills neighborhood, overlooking the city's downtown and the Kanawha River. For 30 years, Sunrise served as a museum, an art gallery and center of social gatherings. In 2002, the Sunrise Museum moved to its new downtown location at the Clay Center for the Arts and Sciences. Sunrise subsequently was sold to a Charleston law firm, which undertook an extensive restoration and modernization.

"SUNRISE" HOME OF EX-GOV. W. A. MacCORKLE, CHARLESTON, W. VA.

Built as a Depression-era public works project at a cost of $3.5 million, Charleston's six-mile-long Kanawha Boulevard carries the Midland Trail/U.S. 60 along the north side of the Kanawha River through the city's downtown. Completed in 1940, the roadway was for a time the most modern in the state. In his *Buildings of West Virginia*, architectural historian S. Allen Chambers Jr. notes, "its construction required the demolition of a number of buildings whose rear elevations, backing onto the river, had long been a source of civic embarrassment."

Kanawha Boulevard from Kanawha City Bridge showing Capitol Dome, Charleston, W. Va.

The West Virginia State Capitol. CHARLESTON, W. VA.

When West Virginia joined the union in 1863, Wheeling became the state capital. State government was later moved to Charleston, then back to Wheeling. In 1877, the Legislature asked the state's voters to decide on a permanent site. They choose Charleston, and this elaborate Capitol building was built. Its 85 rooms housed not just the Legislature and the governor's office but the entirety of state government. In 1921, the Capitol burned and the state moved into temporary makeshift quarters, dubbed the "Cardboard Capitol." Ironically, it too would be destroyed by fire in 1927.

State Capitol from across the great Kanawha River, Charleston, W. Va.   33

Within days of the 1921 Capitol fire, the state began making plans for a new Capitol. The burned Capitol had stood downtown on Capitol Street (hence the street's name) and many people favored rebuilding at the original site. Instead, a tract of land overlooking the Kanawha River in the city's east end was selected. The state commissioned Cass Gilbert, one of the nation's best-known architects, to design the new Capitol building. It was built in stages over a period of years, with the last portion, topped by a soaring gold-covered dome, dedicated in 1932. The Capitol cost $10 million to build and many thought it outrageous for the state to spend that kind of money on a building at a time when West Virginians, like other Americans, were coping with the ravages of the Great Depression, but the money proved a wise investment. The majestic structure has served the state well and each year attracts thousands of admiring visitors.

The official residence for West Virginia's governors faces the Kanawha River on a site just west of the Capitol. It was built in 1924-25, while the Capitol was still under construction. The mansion's architect, Walter F. Martens of Charleston, worked closely with the Capitol's architect, Cass Gilbert. The main floor houses the public rooms that welcome tours and all manner of functions. The second and third floors provide private living quarters for the state's governors and their families.

Located on Kanawha Boulevard just west of the Governor's Mansion, Holly Grove Mansion was built in 1815 by Daniel Ruffner, a member of the family that pioneered the salt industry in the Kanawha Valley and went on to play an important role in the region's commercial and political affairs. Holly Grove was originally a working plantation with a number of barns and other outbuildings spread across an open

expanse where the State Capitol and Executive Mansion now stand. Located as it was on the James River & Kanawha Turnpike, the Ruffner House became a popular stop for travelers. The mansion gained its present day appearance around 1902 when a new owner, John Nash, added the monumental front portico. The house is now owned by the state and is officially part of the Capitol Complex. It was occupied by the West Virginia Commission on Aging from 1979 to 2005. Vacant since that time, it has been allowed to sadly deteriorate. A multi-million dollar restoration is planned.

State Office Building Number Three, Charleston, West Virginia

Although Cass Gilbert's three-unit Capitol was intended to serve all of the state's governmental needs, it quickly proved inadequate. And in 1949, this office building was constructed at the Capitol Complex. Designed by the famed architect's son, Cass Gilbert Jr., the building's design effectively complements that of the Capitol. Officially, it's designated State Office Building Number Three, but it's generally called the "Department of Motor Vehicles building." In more recent years, additional buildings have been constructed at the complex and a number of memorials now dot the grounds.

Completed at the Capitol Complex in 1976, the Culture Center was built, in the words of Governor Arch Moore, to be a "West Virginia treasure house," containing a theater, the state archives and a museum chronicling the state's history. The long-closed museum reopened in 2009 after a $17.3 million makeover that continues to draw rave reviews from visitors.

The stockade built by George Clendenin and his fellow settlers served as the first courthouse in Kanawha County. In 1796, a one-story log structure was built as the county's first "official" courthouse. A second log building next door housed a two-cell jail (one cell reserved for debtors, the second cell for all other prisoners) and an apartment for the jailer's family. At the back of the jail stood a whipping post. In 1817, the log structure was replaced by a two-story brick building that was used until the first part of the existing courthouse was built in 1892. When the original courthouse was built, Kanawha Boulevard was known as Front Street and the courthouse entrance faced Front Street and the river. Later, when Virginia Street became a main road and river traffic declined, the entrance was changed to face Virginia.

Court House, Charleston, W. Va.

Charleston's City Hall, built in 1921-22, stands on the southeast corner of Virginia and Court streets. A classical Beaux-Arts building, it was designed by Charleston architect H. Rus Warne, who gave the city many of its finest structures. This vintage postcard view of the building was mailed in 1926.

CITY HALL, CHARLESTON, W. VA.

The arrival of the Chesapeake & Ohio Railway in 1873 on the south side of the Kanawha River and the 1884 completion of the Kanawha & Ohio (later renamed the Kanawha & Michigan) on the river's north side linked Charleston with the nation's growing rail network. The C&O opened this impressive looking passenger depot in 1905. It remains in use by Amtrak today. The stately old building also houses a restaurant and offices for a private business.

Chesapeake and Ohio Railway Passenger Station, Charleston, W. Va.

K. & M. Depot, Charleston, W. Va.

The Kanawha & Michigan Railroad built this red brick Charleston depot in 1897. Located at the front of Broad Street, it marked the line of demarcation between the city's residential and industrial districts. The abandoned depot was demolished in 1975. Today, the site is the home of the city's popular Capitol Market.

This 1920 postcard provides a splendid view of downtown Charleston as seen from the south side of the Kanawha River. The tall building at the far left is the Union Building. Erected in 1911, it was once the tallest building in West Virginia. The structure, one of the city's best known landmarks, is still used as an office building, but the construction of Kanawha Boulevard cut it off from the rest of the downtown, leaving it a lonely sentinel on the river.

BIRD'S EYE VIEW OF BUSINESS SECTION, CHARLESTON, W. VA.

Charleston's 3,500-seat Municipal Auditorium was built in 1939 as a Depression era Works Project Administration (WPA) undertaking. It is still used for various entertainment events.

PORTFOLIO:
The Charleston Hotels of Yesteryear

Travelers on the Midland Trail/U.S. 60 often spent the night in Charleston before they continued their journey. When they did so they had their choice of a wide range of hotels, with rates to fit most every pocketbook. Here's a glimpse of some downtown Charleston hotels from yesteryear—all of them long since gone.

The Fleetwood Hotel on Capitol Street had a café on the ground floor and nickelodeon next door. "Harry," the sender of this card in 1910, wanted "Ruth" to know that he would "be back some time next week." In the early 1930s, the Fleetwood housed the studios of Charleston's first radio station, WOBU. The station later changed its call letters to WCHS.

Fleetwood Hotel, Charleston, W.Va.

Kanawha Hotel, Charleston, W. Va.

Demolished in 2003, the Kanawha Hotel was a Charleston landmark for 100 years. People once called it the best place to eat between White Sulphur Springs and Cincinnati. John F. Kennedy celebrated his victory in the 1960 West Virginia presidential primary in the hotel ballroom. The grand old hotel is shown here on a card postmarked in 1908.

ON THE BANKS OF THE GREAT KANAWHA RIVER   95971

Giant trees partially obscure this postcard view of the Ruffner Hotel. At the turn of the last century, the eight-story Ruffner was not only Charleston's biggest hotel but also its best. The stately old hotel fell to the wrecking ball in 1970. Note the type at the top of the card identifying the hotel's location—"On the Midland Trail."

Many of this book's readers may not be old enough to recall the golden age of luggage labels—roughly 1900 to the 1950s—when hotels used the labels as advertising, slapping them on suitcases, steamer trunks and all kinds of bags. Today, they're highly collectable. This vintage label promoted Charleston's Daniel Boone Hotel. The Boone, which opened in 1929, was always a busy place, but never more so than when the West Virginia Legislature was in session. For years, the hotel was the unofficial headquarters for legislators and lobbyists alike. Long closed as a hotel, the structure was converted into an office building.

Today's travelers who visit downtown Charleston will find much that would have amazed those who visited the city only a few decades ago. The Town Center mall, shown here, offers three stories of shopping and dining. The West Virginia Power attracts baseball fans to Appalachian Power Park each summer. And the Clay Center for the Arts & Sciences is a year-round delight, with two floors of kid-friendly interactive science exhibits, a planetarium, a fine arts museum and a theater that is home to the West Virginia Symphony.

SOUTH CHARLESTON

South Charleston is the site of the second-largest remaining Indian burial mound in West Virginia. The largest is the Grave Creek Mound found in—not surprisingly—Moundsville in the state's northern panhandle. The South Charleston Mound is a large earthen pile measuring 175 feet in diameter at its base and standing approximately 25 feet high. It's hard to miss, as it's located in the heart of the city's downtown business district along MacCorkle Avenue (the Midland Trail/U.S. 60), fronting Oakes Avenue and 7th Avenue. The property, shown here in a vintage postcard view, was deeded to the city in 1931 for use as a public park. Previously, P.W. Criel owned the property, thus the site was long known as the "Criel Mound."

Historic Indian Mound, South Charleston, W. Va.

Archeologists credit construction of the mound to Indians of the Adena Culture. But most people simply refer to them as the "Mound Builders." The mound was constructed, the experts say, somewhere between about 250-150 B.C. In 1883-84, the Smithsonian Institution sent a party of archeologists to excavate the mound. They found a dozen or so skeletons, a flint lance head, copper bracelets, arrowheads, tools and various metal and shell ornaments. All are now part of the Smithsonian's collection in Washington, D.C. Visitors willing to exercise their legs a bit can climb to the top of the mound via a set of stone steps that start at a stone and steel archway.

Located at 313 D Street, the South Charleston Interpretive Center offers informative exhibits about the city's famous mound, the Midland Trail and the region's long-time role as "Chemical Capitol of the World." The center opened in 2009, jointly funded by the federal and state governments and the city of South Charleston, in cooperation with the Midland Trail Scenic Highway Association.

Next door to the South Charleston Interpretive Center is the LaBelle Theater, with its restored Art Deco style marquee.

With the advent of World War I, the former farmland in the Kanawha Valley sprouted several chemical production operations, including the sprawling Union Carbide plant in South Charleston. Today the plant is operated by the Dow Chemical Co., which remains one of the community's largest employers.

SIDE TRIP: Dunbar, Institute and Nitro

West of Charleston, the Midland Trail/U.S. 60 runs along the south bank of the Kanawha River. Travelers who take a side trip north across the river can visit the communities of Dunbar, Institute and Nitro.

Dunbar was named for Mary Dunbar, who inherited land from George Washington. Dunbar was a farming community until the arrival of the glass and chemical industries in the early 1900s. Dunbar has several parks, including Wine Cellar Park, with its three large restored stone walk-in wine cellars. The cellars were built before the Civil War and are said to have been used to hide runaway slaves.

Institute is the home of West Virginia State University. The school was established as the West Virginia Colored Institute in 1891 under the second Morrill Act, which provided for land-grant institutions for black students in the 17 states that had segregated schools. Booker T. Washington, the noted black educator, was instrumental in having the school located in the Kanawha Valley. He visited the campus often and spoke at its first commencement exercise.

West Virginia Colored Institute, Institute, W. Va.

Over the years, the school would undergo several name changes, eventually becoming West Virginia State College. It enrolled its first white students in 1954-55 and by 1959 the school had more white students than black students. In 2004, the school gained university status. Today, it has more than 5,200 students and more than 80 academic programs. The Alumni Carillon, shown here, is a familiar landmark on the campus.

The community of Nitro was named for the nitrocellulose used in gunpowder—a name that was certainly logical for a town built to house workers at a huge gunpowder plant ordered built by the U.S. government during World War I. Within less than a year, thousands of construction workers built not only the plant but also a brand-new town to house its employees. Barracks were built to house unmarried workers, but individual homes were built for those with families. This 1918 photo shows a street of six-room bungalows built for plant executives. Ironically, the first load of gunpowder shipped from the plant was also its last, as the war ended before it could get into full production. After the war, the government sold the plant to the Charleston Industrial Corp., which set about recruiting chemical-related industries to use portions of it. Today, Nitro remains a center of chemical production.

ST. ALBANS

Back on the south side of the Kanawha, the Midland Trail/U.S. 60 runs along the riverbank through the city of St. Albans. A roadside marker notes that George Washington originally owned 2,000 acres of land along the Kanawha and Coal rivers, a tract that included the present-day site of downtown St. Albans.

St. Albans Roadside Park offers a playground, picnic facilities, a boat ramp and this missile display, dedicated in honor of famed flying ace Chuck Yeager, the West Virginia native who in 1947 became the first man to fly faster than the speed of sound. The missile, painted red, white and blue, seems poised for takeoff.

Venture off the Midland Trail/U.S. 60 for a few blocks and there's much to see and appreciate in historic downtown St. Albans. Here's a vintage postcard, showing the town as it might have appeared to visitors circa 1908.

PHOTO. BY R. J. KRAMER   MAIN STREET, LOOKING EAST, ST. ALBANS, W. VA.

Recently restored, the C&O Depot in St. Albans is fronted by one of the city's original brick streets. The yellow color was standard for the C&O's depots for many years. The numerous tall windows, high ceilings and extended roof overhangs mark the building as architecturally distinctive.

Prominent lumberman and civic leader William E. Mohler built this handsome home in 1901. The old house is one of two-dozen stops on a walking tour of the St. Albans Main Street Historic District.

The Alban Theater opened in 1938. Many local residents can recall that their first movie, their first date or maybe even their first kiss took place at the Alban. Now the former Art Deco-style movie house has been transformed into the Alban Arts and Conference Center.

PUTNAM COUNTY

Located between West Virginia's two largest cities, Charleston and Huntington, the southern portion of Putnam County is fast becoming a bedroom for the two communities, while much of the northern portion of the county remains farmland and woodland.

Created in 1848 from parts of Cabell and Kanawha counties to the south, and Mason County to the north, Putnam County was named for Israel Putnam, who was a hero in the French and Indian War and later a general in the Revolutionary War.

The Midland Trail/U.S. 60 cuts across the southern portion of the county.

HURRICANE

It was a cold, misty morning in the year 1774. A party of surveyors, commissioned by George Washington, traveled down the Kanawha River. When the surveyors encountered a small creek, they noted in their journal that all the trees at the mouth of the creek were bent in the same direction, apparently laid low by a massive storm. Thus, they called the location, the "place of the hurricane." And the creek became known as Hurricane Creek.

Hurricane Bridge, shown on maps of Virginia as early as 1811, was located about one mile north of Hurricane's present-day downtown. Hurricane Creek crossed the James River & Kanawha Turnpike (the future Midland Trail/U.S. 60) and the creek was too deep for the stage and other conveyances to ford, so a sturdy bridge was built. A small community grew up, consisting of several homes, a general store, a log building used for church services, school classes and public meetings and a tavern that provided food, drink and a bed (of sorts) for stagecoach travelers. This painting of a stagecoach making its way to Hurricane Bridge is one of a half dozen colorful murals that decorate buildings in downtown Hurricane.

The coming of the Chesapeake & Ohio Railway in 1873 caused the town to be slightly relocated and its name changed to Hurricane Station. The railroad caused the town to grow with the building of stores and hotels, and in 1888 it was incorporated as Hurricane. This mural commemorates the all-important arrival of the C&O in the community.

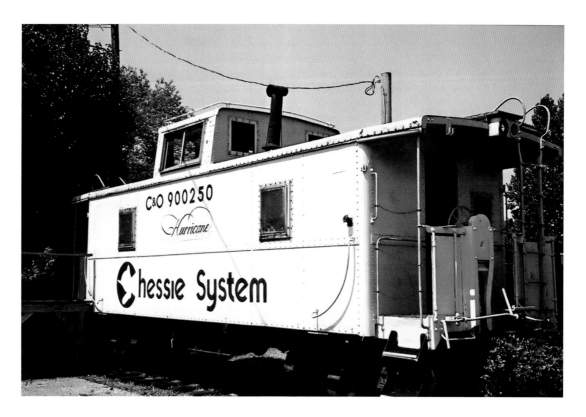

A retired Chessie System caboose on Main Street now houses a mini-museum, a recognition of the important role the railroad played in the city's growth and development.

The Hurricane Volunteer Department is recognized by a mural on its building on Main Street. The department dates back to 1896 when a group of concerned citizens banded together to provide fire protection for the community. The department was officially incorporated in 1949. This illustration details just one portion of the large mural that chronicles the department's growth over the years.

Designated "History Row," Hurricane's Main Street boasts more than a dozen specialty shops offering one-of-kind antiques, gifts and collectibles. A gazebo, constructed on the site on the town's old C&O depot, invites visitors to stop and linger a while.

Rappold's Barber Shop has been a fixture in downtown Hurricane since 1908. Four generations of Rappold men have been cutting the hair of generations of customers.

The oldest continuously operating business in Hurricane is the *Putnam Breeze* newspaper, which was established in 1910. The first owner, publisher and editor was James E. Billups. In 1913, the weekly publication was sold to Robert F. Forth, whose descendents still own it. Here's a portion of the mural capturing a scene in the paper's Putnam Avenue offices in days gone by. The man in the hat is seated at a Linotype, a clattering type-setting machine long since banished from the nation's newspaper offices, replaced by computerized type-setting systems.

CABELL COUNTY

Cabell County, formed from part of Kanawha County in 1809, was named in honor of Virginia Governor William H. Cabell.

In the county's earliest years, its largest communities were Barboursville and Guyandotte. But that all changed when rail tycoon Collis P. Huntington purchased a mostly vacant tract of river bottom along the Ohio just downstream from Guyandotte, and there, in 1871, set about erecting the town that is his namesake.

CULLODEN

Culloden, located on the Midland Trail/U.S. 60 astride the Putnam-Cabell County line, dates back to a tavern that opened in 1818 and was burned by Union troops in the Civil War. In the 1890s, when Capt. B.H. Justice wanted to open a saloon and the county refused to issue him a license, he got around that by having the town incorporated. Interest in the municipal corporation soon lapsed, however, and Culloden reverted to being unincorporated.

MIDWAY BETWEEN CHARLESTON AND HUNTINGTON ON ROUTE 60

OA3180

J. J. JIMISON TOURIST CAMP, CULLODEN, W. VA.

In the era before the advent of modern roadside motels, the J. J. Jimison Tourist Camp was located in Culloden. This undated vintage postcard boasted that it was located "Midway between Charleston and Huntington on Route 60" and had all the latest conveniences, including running water and electric lights.

MILTON

An early settlement grew up here at the Mud River crossing of the James River & Kanawha Turnpike. When the town was incorporated in 1876 it was named for Milton Reese, a large landowner and Milton's first postmaster. Over the years it developed as a regional commercial and small-scale industrial center. The entire business section burned in 1911, and today's commercial buildings were built after the fire. Local residents often describe themselves as being from "Milton on the Mud," a reference to the usually tame Mud River that sometimes spills out of its banks and sends folks heading for higher ground. This postcard reproduces a picture of Milton dated 1884.

PICTURE OF MILTON, W. VA., IN 1884.

This vintage postcard, mailed in 1939, shows Milton's Main Street as it would have appeared to a visiting traveler in that era. Curiously, the card shows only one automobile, parked far down the street. Either it was a really slow day in downtown Milton or the retouch artist who enhanced the card by adding the blue sky and puffy white clouds also decided to remove any other cars or trucks included in the original photo.

Milton is perhaps best known as the home of the world-famous Blenko Glass Company, manufacturers of widely collected glassware, stained glass used for church windows and fine leaded glass used in historic restorations. William Blenko had operated a glass factory in England and in 1923 came to this country for the express purpose of setting up a glass operation. The presence of the C&O Railway and a good supply of natural gas prompted him to establish his factory in Milton. The company remains a family-run enterprise.

In 1966, Blenko built an attractive Visitor Center, where glass lovers can browse the first-floor gift shop and tour a second-floor museum with examples of glass artistry on display.

Colorful glass panels decorate a fence at the Blenko Visitor Center.

Originally Blenko made only sheet glass, but with the coming of the Great Depression and the resultant lessening of demand for new or replacement windows, the company started making the colorful hand-blown vases, pitchers and other glassware for which it has become internationally known. (*Herald-Dispatch* photo.)

A short walk away from the Blenko gift shop is an observation area where visitors can watch the company's skilled craftsmen at work. (*Herald-Dispatch* photo.)

Said to have been built in 1876, the old covered bridge at Milton is one of Cabell County's best-known landmarks. The well-built bridge carried vehicular traffic on Cabell County 25 until 1985, when old age finally caught up with it and the span's deterioration prompted highway officials to limit its use to pedestrians only.

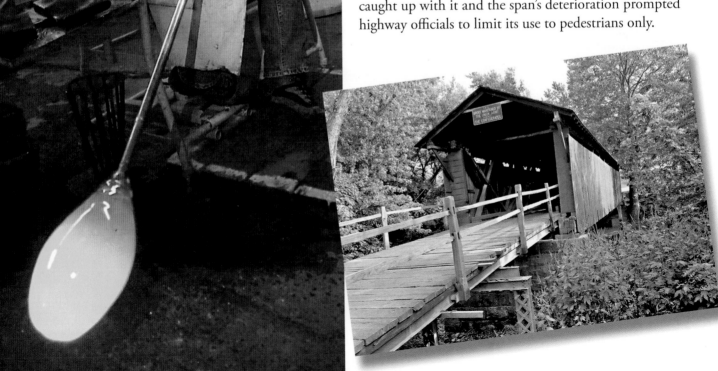

A new bridge was built upstream in 1991, and the old span was closed even to pedestrians in 1996. Plans were made to move the bridge to a nearby site where the James River & Kanawha Turnpike had crossed the river via another covered bridge, long ago demolished. Instead, however, the bridge was moved to a location that provides the public greater opportunity to see and enjoy it. It now spans a lake at Pumpkin Park, scene of two big annual events—Milton's Pumpkin Festival and the Cabell County Fair.

Not every little town can boast that it has its own jet plane, but Milton can make that claim. There's no marker on the seven-foot pedestal that supports this Air Force F-86D Sabre jet but anyone in town can tell you it's a memorial to those from Milton who died serving their country. Dedicated in 1962, the jet was put in its place of honor by Milton American Legion Post 139.

MORRIS MEMORIAL CONVALESCENT & NURSING HOME
MILTON, W. VA.

Walter T. Morris, a bachelor farmer who lived near Milton, was plunged into despair in 1928 when his niece developed polio. Fortunately, she recovered. But her plight had such a profound impact on Moore that in 1930 he deeded his 200-acre farm for use as a polio hospital. At first, the old farmhouse housed a handful of patients. But in the 1930s, the federal Works Progress Administration constructed an impressive stone building that housed an up-to-date hospital. Later, when the development of the Salk vaccine dramatically decreased the number of polio cases, the building was converted into a nursing home. The nursing home closed in 2009.

Union Baptist Church, located at 1295 James River & Kanawha Turnpike in Milton, was originally built as a log structure in 1788. In 1849, the congregation built a new church at an adjacent site. With the coming of the Civil War, Union troops were garrisoned at the church to deny the Confederate troops the use of a turnpike bridge that stood there. The soldiers left the church in shambles. It was restored after the war, but bayonet marks and bullet-pock marks can still be seen in the walls.

BARBOURSVILLE

Barboursville, located near the junction of the Mud and Guyandotte rivers, was founded in 1813 and named for James Barbour, who was governor of Virginia at the time. In 1835, a visitor described it as a "handsome little village" of "25 dwelling houses." In its early years, the village not only was a retail center but also had small factories that produced furniture, hats, wagons and buggies, as well as a sawmill, tanner and harness maker. The James River & Kanawha Turnpike ran straight through the little town. A side road connected the turnpike to the nearby village of Guyandotte.

During the Civil War, Barboursville was the scene of at least two skirmishes. Shown here, in a sketch done by an unidentified artist in November of 1861, is the entrance into the town of a unit of the Union Army—the 34th Regiment of the Ohio Volunteers. The building at right of center was then the Cabell County Courthouse.

Confederate raids eventually made it necessary to move the county seat to nearby Guyandotte. At the war's end, it was moved back to Barboursville but in 1887, with Huntington now the center of business activity in the county, it was moved to Huntington. At that point, the former courthouse became home to, briefly, the Barboursville Seminary and then, when that venture failed, Barboursville College.

BARBOURSVILLE COLLEGE,
BARBOURSVILLE, W. VA.
1889.

Morris Harvey College Campus, Barboursville, W. Va.

By 1900, Barboursville College was all but bankrupt, but wealthy West Virginia businessman Morris Harvey and his wife Rose came to the struggling school's rescue, paying off all its debts and helping it build brick dormitories and a gymnasium. To thank the Harveys, the school's trustees renamed it Morris Harvey College. This vintage postcard showing the campus was postmarked in 1909.

Morris and Rose Harvey dreamed of moving the struggling college to Charleston but didn't live to see that happen. Their dream of a Charleston campus wasn't realized until 1947. This hand-colored postcard from 1912 shows the front veranda at Rose Harvey Hall on the Barboursville campus.

BARBOURSVILLE, W. VA.
The Front Veranda or Promenade,
Rose Harvey Hall, Morris
Harvey College

When U.S. 60 was built, the road crews bypassed Barboursville, thus sparing it the kind of commercial development that undoubtedly would have swept away many of the period structures that line both sides of the village's Main Street, which follows the route of the old James River & Kanawha Turnpike. The Thornburg family operated a store for 75 years in this brick building on the corner of Barboursville's Central Avenue and Main Street. When this photograph was shot in the 1940s, the old building, which was once

used as stagecoach stop on the turnpike, was home to the L.& H. Dairy Bar. The next building over was the M.C. Johnson Drugstore.

This small log house originally housed a toll collector who collected a fee from those turnpike travelers who wished to take the ferry that crossed the Guyandotte River. The Daughters of the American Revolution rebuilt the structure at its current site in 1950 and it now serves as their museum and meeting place.

With the departure of Morris Harvey College from its hilltop campus, the Cabell County school system took over the buildings on the lower section of the hill and the state located a mental hospital in the buildings at the top of the hill. The hospital was closed in the 1970s and in 1981, after a long campaign by organizations representing the state's veterans, the vacant complex was dedicated as the West Virginia Veterans Home. The bricked area in the lower portion of this photograph marks the site of the former Cabell County Courthouse, Morris Harvey College and Barboursville Junior High School.

Located on Martha Road, the 900-acre Barboursville Park includes soccer fields, three baseball fields, tennis courts, basketball courts, volleyball courts, Little League baseball fields, a midget football field, fishing lakes and ponds, picnic areas, a 1,000-person amphitheater, walking trails, a horse show ring and an archery range.

Located along the Midland Trail/U.S. 60 between Barboursville and Huntington is one of the oddest sights to be seen along the historic road—a genuine pink elephant. The building it stands in front of once housed a gift shop but today is occupied by an insurance agency. The elephant, however, remains. A few years ago, some Marshall University fans got carried away and painted it green but it was soon restored to its original hue.

GUYANDOTTE

Guyandotte, located where the Guyandotte River flows into the Ohio, was a thriving little village long before rail tycoon Collis P. Huntington arrived on the scene and established the town that carries his name. The new town of Huntington, established in 1871, quickly eclipsed Guyandotte and in 1911 its citizens voted to become part of Huntington. But Guyandotte remains proud of its history and there's no better symbol of that pride than the Madie Carroll House. Originally built in Gallipolis, Ohio, in the early 1790s, the house was floated down the Ohio on a flatboat in 1810, the same year Guyandotte was founded. Operated as an inn for many years, the old house is being restored by the Madie Carroll House Preservation Society. Tours are offered by appointment.

For decades the location of the proposed East Huntington Bridge was the subject of stormy controversy, with a long list of possible sites proposed, debated and ultimately rejected. Ironically, when the bridge was finally built at 31st Street and opened to traffic in 1985, it proved to be a thing of beauty. Indeed, its dramatic design soon made it a Huntington landmark. The 2,841-foot bridge is a cable-stayed, concrete span with a single pylon that rises 370 feet in the air over the Ohio River. The silhouette of the single tower with its suspension cables outlined against the sky is truly striking.

HUNTINGTON

The citizens of Guyandotte were sure that Collis P. Huntington would select their little village to be the western terminus of his Chesapeake & Ohio Railway. Instead, Huntington purchased a tract of level land on the Ohio River just downstream from Guyandotte and there set about building an entirely new town. An early visitor to Huntington reported finding eight churches, four hotels "and a generous number of saloons."

Today's visitor to Huntington will find much to see and do. Pullman Square, with its retail stores, restaurants and cineplex, stands downtown on 3rd Avenue, the historic route of the Midland Trail/ U.S. 60 through the city. Just steps away are the Big Sandy Superstore Arena, Harris Riverfront Park and Heritage Village. Elsewhere the Huntington Museum of Art and the Heritage Farm Museum and Village beckon fun-seekers.

Marshall University's campus lies astride the Midland Trail/ U.S. 60. The campus is bounded by 3rd and 5th Avenues on the north and south, and Hal Greer Boulevard and 22nd Street on the east and west. This giant sculpture on the wall of Joan C. Edwards Stadium commemorates the tragic 1970 plane crash that claimed the lives of the Marshall football team. The 2008 movie "We Are Marshall" told the story of the crash and the school's amazing comeback from that tragedy.

When the county seat was moved from Barboursville to Huntington, the county government initially shared use of the city building. However, the county immediately purchased a square block of land for a new courthouse. Financial problems delayed its construction but it was completed in 1901. A west wing was added in 1923 and an east wing in 1940. This vintage postcard shows the building after the completion of the two wings.

In 1911, when Huntington's city fathers purchased a tract of land at 5th Avenue and 8th Street for construction of a new City Hall, they paid the unheard-of sum of $46,000. The King Lumber Co. won the construction contract with a bid of $115,380. The architect was Verus T. Ritter, who also designed many of early Huntington's other fine buildings. The building has changed little since its completion in 1915.

Here's Huntington's 4th Avenue as it would have appeared to a visiting traveler in the late 1920s or early 1930s. The tall building at the left is the former First Huntington National Bank Building. The tall building in the center of the card is the West Virginia Building, at one time the tallest in the state.

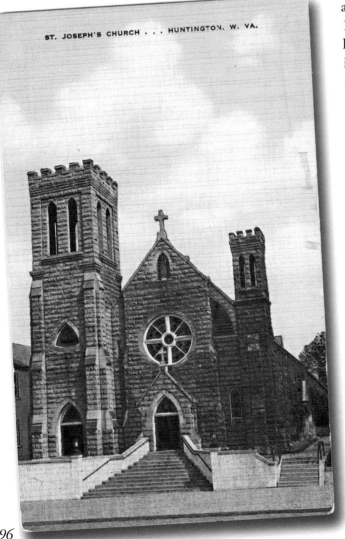

ST. JOSEPH'S CHURCH . . . HUNTINGTON, W. VA.

Huntington is sometimes called "The City of Churches," and certainly it boasts a good many. Just a few blocks of the downtown are home to eight congregations, including St. Joseph's Catholic Church, a Gothic Revival design done in light-toned sandstone. The foundation for the church was laid in 1884 and its construction completed in 1889.

96

PORTFOLIO:
The Huntington Hotels of Yesteryear

Weary travelers arriving in Huntington and seeking a bed for the night had a wide range of hotels to pick from, including these.

The Scranage, a two-story frame building erected in 1872, is said to have been Huntington's first hotel. Other pre-1900 hotels included the Ware and the Breslin. But the premier hotels in the city's early years were the Adelphi and, shown here in a vintage postcard view, the Florentine, which opened in 1887. It was demolished in 1933.

Florentine Hotel, Huntington, W. Va.

The 13-story, 300-room Prichard Hotel, built by developer Fred C. Prichard, opened at 6th Avenue and 9th Street in 1926. This postcard view is undated but appears to be from the 1940s when, as the card boasts, six floors of the hotel had been "completely air conditioned." Prichard also constructed the nearby Robson-Prichard office building. The Prichard Hotel ceased operation in 1970. Today, the building houses offices and apartments.

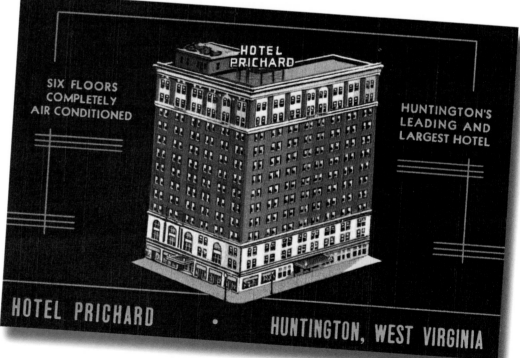

HOTEL PRICHARD

SIX FLOORS COMPLETELY AIR CONDITIONED

HUNTINGTON'S LEADING AND LARGEST HOTEL

HOTEL PRICHARD · HUNTINGTON, WEST VIRGINIA

Built at a cost of $400,000, Huntington's grand Frederick Hotel welcomed its first guests in 1906. Its construction is said to have required 3.5 million bricks, 4,000 electric lights, 282 miles of electrical wire, 200 telephones and 5 railroad cars of glass. This postcard view was mailed in 1924. The Frederick closed as a hotel in 1973. Today, the building houses offices and apartments.

Like many other major hotels of the day, the Frederick offered guests a broad range of services, including this well-equipped barbershop, shown on a vintage postcard. Six barber chairs suggest what must have been a busy trade.

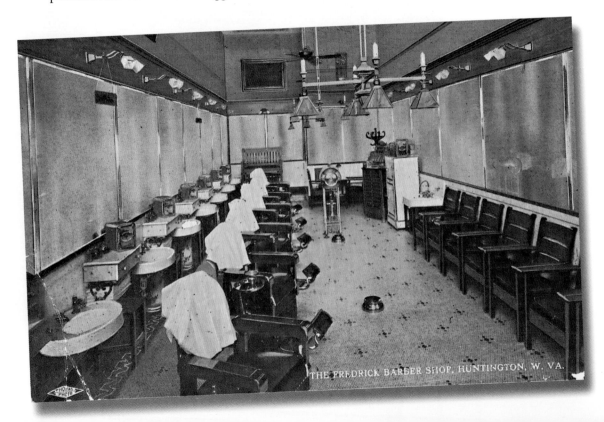

THE FREDERICK BARBER SHOP, HUNTINGTON, W. VA.

Established in 1913, Huntington's Ritter Park is a recreation mecca for people throughout the Tri-State Area. The 70-acre park has a walking trail that borders Four Pole Creek, an award-winning children's playground, a 1,000-seat amphitheater that can be used for small concerts and plays, an internationally known Rose Garden, and a tennis center with eleven outdoor tennis courts and four indoor courts.

Just west of Ritter Park lies Memorial Park, the setting for Huntington's Memorial Arch. Dedicated on Armistice Day in 1924, the arch was constructed as a memorial to the soldiers from Cabell County who perished in World War I but since has come to memorialize all those who have fallen in the nation's wars. The arch is a quarter-scale replica of the famed Arch-de-Triumph in Paris.

Built in 1928, Huntington's Keith-Albee was sometimes described as a "Million Dollar Temple of Amusement." In fact, the cost of the theater soared from an initial budget of $250,000 to an eventual $2 million, a result of its lavish interior décor. Designed by Thomas Lamb, the premier theater architect of the great age of movie palaces, the Keith seats an audience of 3,000. At the time, that made it second in size only to the Roxy in New York City. (*Herald-Dispatch* photo.)

In 2006 the Keith-Albee Theatre closed as a functioning movie theater and its owners, the Hyman family, donated the old theater to the Marshall University Foundation, Inc., who in turn passed it on to the newly-formed Keith-Albee Performing Arts Center Foundation. Today the Keith continues as the home of the Marshall Artists Series and other special events, and is gradually being restored to it former grandeur.

Located just west of downtown Huntington on the Midland Trail/U.S. 60, Central City was a separate community with its own mayor, council, police force and fire department from 1893 to 1909, before bowing to the inevitable and agreeing to be annexed by Huntington. Central City was once known as a manufacturing center, but the factories are long gone. An exception is Heiner's Bakery. Established in 1905, today it's a major regional bakery. Today, Central City is best known for its many antique shops and the fresh produce sold each summer at the Central City Market.

WAYNE COUNTY

While Huntington is the county seat of Cabell County, the west end of the city lies in Wayne County. Formed in 1842 from Cabell County, Wayne is West Virginia's westernmost county and thus the last county that the Midland Trail/U.S. 60 traverses before it crosses the Big Sandy River and enters Kentucky.

The county was named for Anthony Wayne, the famous Revolutionary War general often referred to as "Mad Anthony Wayne" for his fiery temper and his reckless courage during battle.

In the 19th Century timber and farming were Wayne County's economic mainstays, followed by coal in the early 20th Century. Today, most of the county's residents work in Huntington or nearby Ashland, Kentucky.

Camden Park

Just west of Huntington on the Midland Trail/U.S. 60 is a Wayne County landmark that's been attracting fun seekers for more than a century—Camden Park.

The Camden Interstate Railway Co., a streetcar line that connected Huntington and Ashland, opened Camden Park in 1903, naming it for the line's principal investor, Senator Johnson M. Camden of Parkersburg.

Camden Park was one of hundreds of similar amusement parks across the country that were created by streetcar lines as a way of bolstering the number of passengers who rode their trolleys, especially on weekends when business sharply declined as people didn't need to get to their jobs. Today, almost all the nation's other trolley parks have vanished. Camden Park is one of a handful still operating. It's West Virginia's only amusement park.

At first, Camden Park was simply a scenic setting for family picnics and games. But in 1907, the park installed its first amusement ride—its much-loved carousel. By 1910, the number of rides had grown to seven, including a roller coaster. Power for the early rides came from the same cable used by the streetcars.

PORTFOLIO:
Vintage views of Camden Park

Swimming Pool at Camden Park, near Huntington, W. Va.

Here are four postcards with vintage views of Camden Park in its earliest years. A card mailed in 1911 featured the park's swimming pool. None of the folks shown in the card seem dressed to take a dip. Note the row of dressing rooms at the right hand side of the card. A 1912 card showed Camden Park's prehistoric Adena mound. One of the largest in the state, the mound provided a handy location for the park's bandstand. The card showing the park's entrance road was mailed in 1915. The arches over the pathway held light bulbs that illuminated the thoroughfare at night.

Mound view, Camden Park, Huntington, W. Va.

In 1911, the streetcar company hired Col. E.G. Via to manage the facility. Six years later, Via purchased the park from the company and continued to operate it until his death in 1946. That year, John Boylin Sr. purchased the park. Boylin owned and managed the park until 1980 and made many improvements and additions.

Entrance to Camden Park, near Huntington, W. Va.

Birdseye View of Camden Park, Huntington, W. Va.

A "Birdseye View" card mailed in 1910 (above) offered a good look at the park's original roller coaster.

In 1958, Boylin installed the park's Big Dipper roller coaster (right). Today, it's one of only a few wooden coasters still operating. Roller coaster fans from all over the country visit the park to ride it. It's been designated a "Coaster Classic" by American Coaster Enthusiasts, a national organization of roller coaster fans.

Unfortunately, the group of Virginia investors who took control of the park in 1980 let it fall into disrepair. The park was poorly managed, and the investors owed a lot of money, much of it to the Boylin family, who still owned the land. In 1995, with the park one day away from bankruptcy, John Boylin Jr., along with his wife and son, again took it over. Since then, the family has worked hard to restore the park's lost luster, adding new attractions and refurbishing old ones.

CEREDO

Just to the west of Camden Park, the Midland Trail/U.S. 60 enters the little town of Ceredo, where the members of the Ceredo Beautification Committee work hard on attractive projects such as this welcome sign that greets motorists.

A New England abolitionist, Eli Thayer, founded Ceredo in 1857. Thayer was determined to demonstrate the superiority of an economic system that wasn't based on slave labor. He named his new settlement after Ceres, the Greek goddess of grain and harvest. When the Civil War erupted in 1861, Ceredo became a Union stronghold. Unfortunately, the Civil War also brought hard times to the town. Only a handful of the early New England settlers stayed, and the population fell from 500 to 125.

One of the few settlers who remained was Zopher D. Ramsdell, who joined the Union army as a private and came out a captain. After the war, he was placed in charge of resuming the area's mail service and remained with the Post Office Department until his death in 1887. His son followed in his footsteps and was Ceredo postmaster for many years. The Ramsdell family home, built in 1858 on the northeast corner of Ceredo's B and 4th Streets, is thought to have been a stop on the Underground Railroad, housing fugitive slaves from the South until they could cross the Ohio River to freedom on the opposite shore. Today the house has been preserved as a museum, open by appointment.

History buffs who visit Ceredo should stop not only at the Ramsdell house but also make sure their itinerary includes the First Congregational Church on the northeast corner of 1st Street West and C Street. An impressive frame church, it was built in 1885-1886. In his *Buildings of West Virginia* (Oxford, 2004) architectural historian S. Allen Chambers observes: "The presence of this relatively large Congregational church in a small West Virginia community reflects Ceredo's New England heritage."

In 1868, Ceredo's founder Eli Thayer experienced financial difficulties that forced him to sell his interest in the town to his mortgage holder, Charles B, Hoard. A New Yorker, Hoard represented that state in the U.S. House of Representatives (1857-1861). A businessman and inventor, he engaged in the manufacture of portable engines and, during the Civil War, the manufacture of arms for the Union Army. On purchasing Thayer's holdings, he moved to Ceredo and until his death in 1886 devoted most of his energy to developing the town. This map from 1877 reflects a number of changes he imposed on Thayer's original town plan.

CEREDO

WAYNE CO 1ST DIST W VA

Scale 400 Ft. to1Inch

1877

KENOVA

As you head west along the Midland Trail/U.S. 60 you leave Ceredo behind and drive directly into Kenova. Only the locals can tell you where one town stops and the other begins. Most folks in the Huntington area tend to talk about "Ceredo-Kenova" as if it were one place.

Kenova is the largest community in highly rural Wayne County. Its history was shaped in large measure by its location on the Ohio and Big Sandy Rivers where Kentucky, Ohio and West Virginia meet—hence the town's fanciful name. It sounds like it might be the name of an Indian tribe, but in fact it was devised by taking a few letters from each of the three states' names.

No 9157   Timber on Big Sandy, looking down river at Kenova, W. Va.

The town served first as a shipping port for timber floated down the Big Sandy River from the wooded slopes to the south. Later, Kenova would become a manufacturing center for various wood products.

Given Kenova's forest heritage, it's surely not coincidental that many of the city's streets are named for trees. The Midland Trail/U.S. 60 makes its way along Oak Street. Other Kenova street names include Beech, Walnut, Popular and Chestnut. This heavily retouched postcard view offers a glimpse of Kenova's Chestnut Street as it looked circa 1940s.

Chestnut Street, Kenova, W. Va.

11900   N. & W. Railroad Bridge and Ohio River, Near Huntington, W. Va.

The town's founder, L.T. Peck, chose its site because he knew it was where the Norfolk & Western Railroad (N&W) planned to build the first bridge across the Ohio between Cincinnati and Wheeling. The bridge was completed in 1892 and Kenova was incorporated in 1894. This undated vintage postcard shows the bridge and identifies it as being "Near Huntington, W.Va." That may be an accurate statement, but it's not one likely to please the town fathers in Kenova.

Both the Baltimore & Ohio Railroad (B&O) and the Chesapeake & Ohio Railway (C&O) later extended their tracks into Kenova, making it a busy rail hub. It's said that more bituminous coal has passed through Kenova than at any other place in the world. And back in the era when the passenger train was still the way folks traveled any long distance, the N&W, C&O and B&O passenger trains all stopped at Kenova's Union Station. Today, the station is long gone. Gone, too, is the town's former N&W roundhouse and the Glenwood Hotel which once housed weary travelers.

But reminders of Kenova's storied past remain. Among them: Ric and Sandy Griffith's large, frame Queen Anne house at 748 Beech Street. The house, built in 1891 and listed on the National Register of Historic Places, has become nationally— even internationally—known as the "Pumpkin House." Each year at Halloween the Griffiths, aided by an army of volunteer helpers, bedeck the old house with rows and rows of carved orange pumpkins.

One can't help but wonder what Joseph Miller, who built the house, would make of the Halloween display. Miller was president of the Kenova Bank and commissioner of the Internal Revenue Service under President Grover Cleveland, who was a close friend and stayed at the house when he visited the area. Colorful stories about the old house abound. Miller's daughter Lavalette was married there and her wedding present was the Wayne County neighborhood that now bears her name. When wallpapering the living room, Griffith discovered marks indicating the level of water in the house during the 1913 and 1937 floods. Unwilling to cover the marks, he put a picture frame over them and papered around it.

NORTH SIDE OF CHESTNUT STREET, KENOVA, W. VA.

Griffith has also worked hard to restore the family's Kenova drugstore. In the process, he's transformed the Griffith & Feil Pharmacy into a time machine that takes visitors back to a simpler day. Walk in and you'll see a stamped tin ceiling, hardwood floors, dozens of framed historic photos, old booths and a working vintage-era soda fountain. For older customers, the place can't help but bring back memories. It's still a working drugstore—with Griffith behind the counter busily filling prescriptions—but also a miniature museum. Over the years the drugstore has had various locations and ownerships but it's been part of Kenova since 1892 when the N&W arrived in town. A vintage postcard view shows the exterior of the Chestnut Street drugstore as it looked in 1924. (The imposing looking building next door is the former Kenova National Bank.)

Chimney Rock, Kenova, W. Va.

Chimney Rock, an unusual rock formation in Wayne County south of Kenova, fascinated area residents for decades. This postcard view was mailed in 1908. The odd-shaped rock was destroyed during construction of Interstate 64 in the 1960s.

West Virginia's most westerly point, Virginia Point Park is located at the confluence of the Ohio and Big Sandy rivers in Kenova. With views of Ohio and Kentucky, its amenities include overnight campgrounds, boat launching ramp, and a large picnic shelter. This vintage-1950s postcard doesn't show the park facilities—or today's commercial development along the riverbanks.

H-8   TRI-STATE VIEW, SHOWING KENTUCKY, WEST VIRGINIA AND OHIO, NEAR HUNTINGTON, W. VA.

OHIO

WEST VIRGINIA

KENTUCKY

6A-H2081

DREAMLAND SWIMMING POOL, KENOVA, W. VA.

Dreamland Pool is surely Kenova's best-known landmark. Built on the Big Sandy riverbank in 1925, it's been attracting summer fun-seekers ever since. It was grocer J.D. Booth who built the pool. Booth sold ice and house coal and had water wells for his icehouse. Thinking about other businesses that used water, he came up with the idea of a swimming pool. Booth constructed his pool on an imposing scale—125 feet wide and 250 feet long, and graduated from only a few inches at the shallow end to a depth of nine feet at the other. Judging from the design of the cars in this old postcard, this is how the pool must have looked in its earliest years.

Dreamland added a dance pavilion to the roof of the main building in the 1930s. The pavilion (shown at the upper right of this postcard view) quickly became a popular nightspot, attracting crowds to dances featuring musical stars such as Glenn Miller, Benny Goodman and Louis Armstrong, as well as a host of local talent. The building housing the pavilion burned in 1973, while the city of Kenova was negotiating to purchase the pool from its private owners. The deal went through anyway, and the city has operated the pool each summer since 1974.

Dreamland is the last stop on our trip 172-mile westward along the Midland Trail/ U.S. 60 through West Virginia. Once it passes Dreamland, the historic roadway crosses the Big Sandy and heads into Kentucky.

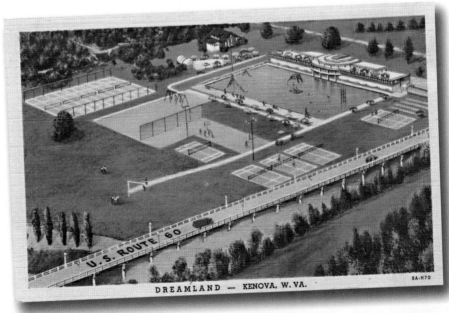

DREAMLAND — KENOVA, W. VA.

James E. Casto

A veteran newspaperman and the author of a number of books on local and regional history, James E. Casto grew up in Huntington, West Virginia, where he graduated from Marshall University, earning a BA in journalism and an MA in English.

Casto was a reporter and editor at *The Herald-Dispatch* in Huntington for more than 40 years before he retired. Active in community affairs, he has taught both journalism and English as a part-time instructor at Marshall. Costumed as Collis P. Huntington, who founded the city of Huntington, he appears at civic clubs, schools and other groups in a first-person program that offers a glimpse of the famed rail tycoon's life and times.

In 2004, Marshall presented him with its John Marshall Medal of Civic Responsibility in recognition of his services to the university and the community. In 2005, the City of Huntington Foundation inducted him as a member of its Greater Huntington Wall of Fame. And in 2006, the Cabell County Public Library named its James E. Casto Local History Room in his honor.

Books by James E. Casto

HUNTINGTON: AN ILLUSTRATED HISTORY (Windsor Publications, 1985) — This is the story of a city born of the Ohio River and the railroad and nurtured by the industrious men and women who have lived and worked there since rail tycoon Collis P. Huntington founded the town in 1870. The narrative is illustrated with more than 100 period black-and-white photographs and a section of color photographs.

TOWBOAT ON THE OHIO (University Press of Kentucky, 1995) — To get a personal look at what it's like to live and work on the Ohio River, the author traveled aboard the towboat *Paul G. Blazer*, from Huntington to Pittsburgh and back. The book introduces readers to the *Blazer's* crew and to the river, while offering a look back at the history of commerce on the busy, hardworking Ohio.

WEST VIRGINIA: MOUNTAIN MAJESTY (West Virginia Division of Culture and History, 1996) — Lavishly illustrated, this handsome coffee-table book isn't as much a history or travel guide as it is "a celebration of the people, places, things and events that have made West Virginia the special place it is."

HUNTINGTON: AN ILLUSTRATED HISTORY – THE MARSHALL UNIVERSITY EDITION (Marshall University Foundation, 1997) — This softbound edition reproduces the text and photographs of the original, out-of-print hardback volume published in 1985, and adds new material to bring the community's story up to date.

CABELL COUNTY (Arcadia, 2001) — A photo history, this book begins with the arrival of the county's first settlers and continues into the 21st century. Some 200 vintage photographs recall key historical events, people and places,

SOUTHERN WEST VIRGINIA: COAL COUNTRY (Arcadia, 2004) — Reproductions of more than 200 vintage postcards offer a nostalgic look at the region's coal mining and the way of life it spawned in the era from 1900 to 1950.

MARSHALL UNIVERSITY (Arcadia, 2005) — Illustrated with more than 200 photographs from the university's archives, this book chronicles the Marshall story, from its humble birth in 1837 to its present role as a major university with 16,000 students.

THE CHESAPEAKE & OHIO RAILWAY (Arcadia, 2006) — A lively history of the C&O from 1785's founding of the predecessor James River Company to 1963, when it merged with the former Baltimore & Ohio Railroad to create the Chessie System (now CSX Transportation).

THE GREAT OHIO RIVER FLOOD OF 1937 (Arcadia, 2009) — This photo history brings together 200 vintage images that chronicle one of the darkest chapters in the region's history.